One HUNDRED Years of Poetry FOR CHILDREN

OXFORD

UNIVERSITY PRESS

Great Clarendon Street, Oxford OX2 6DP

Oxford University Press is a department of the University of Oxford.
It furthers the University's objective of excellence in research, scholarship,
and education by publishing worldwide in

Oxford   New York

Auckland   Cape Town   Dar es Salaam   Hong Kong   Karachi
Kuala Lumpur   Madrid   Melbourne   Mexico City   Nairobi
New Delhi   Shanghai   Taipei   Toronto

With offices in

Argentina   Austria   Brazil   Chile   Czech Republic   France   Greece
Guatemala   Hungary   Italy   Japan   Poland   Portugal   Singapore
South Korea   Switzerland   Thailand   Turkey   Ukraine   Vietnam

Oxford is a registered trade mark of Oxford University Press

in the UK and in certain other countries

Database right Oxford University Press (maker)

First published 1999

First published in this edition 2007

British Library Cataloguing in Publication Data

ISBN 978-0-19-276350-1

9 10

Printed and bound by CPI Group (UK) Ltd, Croydon, CR0 4YY

Paper used in the production of this book is a natural,
recyclable product made from wood grown in sustainable forests.
The manufacturing process conforms to the environmental
regulations of the country of origin.

One HUNDRED Years of Poetry FOR CHILDREN

Michael Harrison &
Christopher Stuart-Clark

OXFORD
UNIVERSITY PRESS

Contents

MYSTERY

library   9
Valerie Worth

The Word Party   10
Richard Edwards

Whatif   11
Shel Silverstein

What's What   12
Alastair Reid

The Boyhood of Dracula   14
Gareth Owen

Not My Day   15
Russell Hoban

The Pancake Collector   16
Jack Prelutsky

The Frog Prince   17
Phoebe Hesketh

Alice and the Frog   18
Brian Morse

A Spell for Midnight   20
Hal Summers

Spell Against Sorrow   21
Kathleen Raine

The Listeners   22
Walter de la Mare

Welsh Incident   24
Robert Graves

Dialogue Between Ghost and
    Priest   26
Sylvia Plath

Mary Celeste   28
Judith Nicholls

Great Black-Backed Gulls   30
John Heath-Stubbs

They Call to One Another   31
George Barker

Everyone Sang   32
Siegfried Sassoon

ANIMALS

The Animals' Arrival   33
Elizabeth Jennings

The Tickle Rhyme   34
Ian Serraillier

The Example   34
W. H. Davies

Considering the Snail   35
Thom Gunn

The Sloth   36
Theodore Roethke

Something Told the Wild Geese
    37
Rachel Field

Don't Call Alligator Long-Mouth
    Till You Cross River   38
John Agard

Trophy   38
Gillian Clarke

We are Going to See the Rabbit
    40
Alan Brownjohn

Song of the Battery Hen   42
Edwin Brock

The Snare   43
James Stephens

Cat's Funeral   44
E. V. Rieu

The Thought-Fox   45
Ted Hughes

Dog Body and Cat Mind   46
Jenny Joseph

Poem   47
William Carlos Williams

Horses on the Camargue   48
Roy Campbell

Horses   50
Edwin Muir

The Donkey   51
G. K. Chesterton

Fetching Cows   52
Norman MacCaig

The Flower-Fed Buffaloes   53
Vachel Lindsay

Caring for Animals   54
Jon Silkin

———————— ❋ ————————

CHILDHOOD

For a Five-year-old   55
Fleur Adcock

It Was Long Ago   56
Eleanor Farjeon

The Game of Life   58
Roy Fuller

When I Was Christened   59
David McCord

Adventures of Isabel   60
Ogden Nash

Father Says   62
Michael Rosen

Playgrounds   63
Berlie Doherty

Where's Everybody?   64
Allan Ahlberg

Truth   65
Barrie Wade

Car Wash   66
Jackie Kay

The Tunnel   67
Brian Lee

Tich Miller   68
Wendy Cope

Televised   69
Maya Angelou

The Shoes   70
John Mole

Into My Heart   72
A. E. Housman

Fern Hill   73
Dylan Thomas

By St Thomas Water   75
Charles Causley

I Wish I Were . . .   77
Rabindranath Tagore

Lost Days   78
Stephen Spender

A Child's Calendar   79
George Mackay Brown

Revelation   80
Liz Lochhead

Unrecorded Speech   81
Anna Adams

A Recollection   82
Frances Cornford

The Lesson   83
Edward Lucie-Smith

Follower 84
Seamus Heaney

The Icing Hand 85
Tony Harrison

Piano 86
D. H. Lawrence

About Friends 87
Brian Jones

Legend 88
Judith Wright

Walking Away 90
C. Day Lewis

---------------- ❋ ----------------

PEOPLE

The Leader 91
Roger McGough

The First Men on Mercury 92
Edwin Morgan

Resurrected 94
Matthew Sweeney

Pitying Heaven 95
Michael Baldwin

About His Person 96
Simon Armitage

Men of Terry Street 97
Douglas Dunn

Every Day in Every Way 98
Kit Wright

The Embankment 99
T. E. Hulme

The Man on the Desert Island
100
Gerda Mayer

Not Waving but Drowning 101
Stevie Smith

Why Brownlee Left 102
Paul Muldoon

Hunger 103
Laurence Binyon

O What is That Sound 104
W. H. Auden

Evans 105
R. S. Thomas

Not My Best Side 106
U. A. Fanthorpe

Old Woman 108
Iain Crichton Smith

Sensitive, Seldom, and Sad 109
Mervyn Peake

The Doomed Spaceman 110
Ted Walker

A Martian Sends a Postcard
Home 111
Craig Raine

---------------- ❋ ----------------

SCENES

For the Record 113
Libby Houston

in Just-spring 114
E. E. Cummings

April Rain Song 115
Langston Hughes

'There Will Come Soft Rains'
115
Sara Teasdale

Day of These Days   116
Laurie Lee

Midsummer, Tobago   117
Derek Walcott

Hard Frost   118
Andrew Young

The Midnight Skaters   119
Edmund Blunden

Fog   120
Carl Sandburg

The More It Snows   120
A. A. Milne

On a Night of Snow   121
Elizabeth Coatsworth

London Snow   122
Robert Bridges

When Skies are Low and Days
    are Dark   123
N. M. Bodecker

The Side Way Back   124
Philip Gross

Southbound on the Freeway   125
May Swenson

The Day the World Ended   126
George MacBeth

Preludes   128
T. S. Eliot

Encounter at St Martin's   130
Ken Smith

Shadows   131
Zaro Weil

Mending Wall   132
Robert Frost

Wall   134
Norman Nicholson

The Old Ships   136
James Elroy Flecker

Posted   138
John Masefield

The Sea   139
James Reeves

Look, No Hands   140
James Berry

※

WAR

Drummer Hodge   141
Thomas Hardy

Abbey Tomb   142
Patricia Beer

The Soldier   144
Rupert Brooke

Newscast   144
Ian Hamilton

My Boy Jack   145
Rudyard Kipling

As the Team's Head-Brass   146
Edward Thomas

Anthem for Doomed Youth
    147
Wilfred Owen

Naming of Parts   148
Henry Reed

Vergissmeinnicht   150
Keith Douglas

Your Attention Please   151
Peter Porter

No More Hiroshimas   153
James Kirkup

Fifteen Million Plastic Bags   155
Adrian Mitchell

In the Desert Knowing Nothing
156
Helen Dunmore

Carriers in the Gulf   157
Alan Ross

A poem about Poems about
Vietnam   158
Jon Stallworthy

Tiananmen   159
James Fenton

The Sunlight on the Garden   160
Louis MacNeice

❋

LOVE

I so liked Spring   161
Charlotte Mew

The River-Merchant's Wife: A
Letter   162
Ezra Pound

Like a Flame   163
Grace Nichols

First Love   164
Brian Patten

Lipservice   164
Max Fatchen

Love Poem   165
Mick Gowar

Any prince to any princess   166
Adrian Henri

A Subaltern's Love-song   168
John Betjeman

Tarantella   170
Hilaire Belloc

Water   172
Robert Lowell

No Sense of Direction   173
Vernon Scannell

Valentine   175
Carol Ann Duffy

The Highwayman   176
Alfred Noyes

An Arundel Tomb   180
Philip Larkin

He Wishes for the Cloths of
Heaven   182
W. B. Yeats

Sometimes   183
Sheenagh Pugh

❋

Index of Titles and First Lines   184
Index of Authors   187
Index of Artists   188
Acknowledgements   189

MYSTERY

library
Valerie Worth

No need even
To take out
A book: only
Go inside
And savour
The heady
Dry breath of
Ink and paper,
Or stand and
Listen to the
Silent twitter
Of a billion
Tiny busy
Black words.

The Word Party
Richard Edwards

Loving words clutch crimson roses,
Rude words sniff and pick their noses,
Sly words come dressed up as foxes,
Short words stand on cardboard boxes,
Common words tell jokes and gabble,
Complicated words play Scrabble,
Swear words stamp around and shout,
Hard words stare each other out,
Foreign words look lost and shrug,
Careless words trip on the rug,
Long words slouch with stooping shoulders,
Code words carry secret folders,
Silly words flick rubber bands,
Hyphenated words hold hands,
Strong words show off, bending metal,
Sweet words call each other 'petal',
Small words yawn and suck their thumbs
Till at last the morning comes.
Kind words give out farewell posies . . .

Snap! The dictionary closes.

Whatif

Shel Silverstein

Last night, while I lay thinking here,
Some Whatifs crawled inside my ear
And pranced and partied all night long
And sang their same old Whatif song:
Whatif I'm dumb in school?
Whatif they've closed the swimming-pool?
Whatif I get beat up?
Whatif there's poison in my cup?
Whatif I start to cry?
Whatif I get sick and die?
Whatif I flunk that test?
Whatif green hair grows on my chest?
Whatif nobody likes me?
Whatif a bolt of lightning strikes me?
Whatif I don't grow taller?
Whatif my head starts getting smaller?
Whatif the fish won't bite?
Whatif the wind tears up my kite?
Whatif they start a war?
Whatif my parents get divorced?
Whatif the bus is late?
Whatif my teeth don't grow in straight?
Whatif I tear my pants?
Whatif I never learn to dance?
Everything seems swell, and then
The night-time Whatifs strike again!

What's What

Alastair Reid

Most people know
the story of how
the frog was a prince
and the dragon was ticklish,
or how the princess
grew fat in the end;
nevertheless,
think of the chance
that the youngest son took—
gloom to the left of him,
groans to the right of him,
no spell to tell him
which way to take,
no map, no book,
no real interest.
All he could say was
'maybe I'm me,'
but he knew not to trust
the wizards who seemed,
the bird with the breast
of too many colours,
the princess who hummed
too perfect a song.
The going was not good,
but his curious head
said over and over
ridiculous words
like *quince* and *Fray Bentos*
all through the wood.

'Yes,' he said firmly,
'nobody pays me,
nobody knows me,
so I will decide
which tree will amaze me
when I see a leaf
I can be sure of.
Whom do I listen to?
Not that toad
with the gem in its head,
nor that mole that mumbles
precise directions,
nor the nice wizard,
so soft and helpful,
nor sweet old women
gathering faggots.
It's that clumsy bird
who looks away,
with only one eye—
untidy feathers,
flying absent-mindedly,
out in all weathers,
little to say—
he's for me.
He's not after
a cut of the treasure.
He knows well
that he's going nowhere
and, what's more,
he doesn't care.

If I'd listened to wizards
and looked in crystals,
I'd be expert
at going wrong;
but I know my birdsong.
Hearing his *tip-tippy*,
I know who *he* is.
I'll go *his* way.'

Needless to say,
the youngest son won
with enough to go on;
and the one-eyed bird,
whoever he was,
went *tip-tip-tippy*
to pleasure his own
well-worn feathers,
over and over,
with no one to hear . . .

Then, one day,
the youngest son
had a youngest son,
and so on.

The Boyhood of Dracula

Gareth Owen

So we let him join us
In the game of Hide and Seek
Because Joanna said we ought,
She being the biggest of us all
And bossy with it.
And him standing there
All hunched and trembling
In the thin snow by the stable door
Watching us like some poor lost soul
With those great eyes he had.
Well, you'd be a thing of stone
To take no pity on the boy.
You never saw a soul
So pale and woebegone;
His pinched nose raw with cold
And naught to keep the bitter wind
The right side of his bones
But that old bit of musty cloak
He always seems to wear.

Poor little mite
You'd think, to watch,
He'd never played the game before.
Maureen Cantelow,
The parson's youngest girl
From Norton Campion way,
She found him straight away
Hardly bothering to hide at all
Among the meal sacks
In the lower barn.

Poor girl,
She must have cut herself
In there somehow
For as I spied them
Running hand in hand below
She sowed fresh seeds of crimson blood
Across ridged and bitter snow.

Not My Day

Russell Hoban

I got up on the wrong side of the day
and came right off; it walked away
showing the whites of its eyes. 'Stop!'
I said, 'I mean to get on top
of you.' It kept on going;
I followed, knowing
days don't always do
exactly what you'd like them to.
'Stand still,' I said, 'I'm going to try again.'
I thought I heard it neigh a little, then
it kept on walking while I stood there talking.
'All right,' I said (it sounded like a threat),
'I'll see you later.' But I haven't yet.

The Pancake Collector

Jack Prelutsky

Come visit my pancake collection,
it's unique in the civilized world.
I have pancakes of every description,
pancakes flaky and fluffy and curled.

I have pancakes of various sizes,
pancakes regular, heavy, and light,
underdone pancakes and overdone pancakes,
and pancakes done perfectly right.

I have pancakes locked up in the closets,
I have pancakes on hangers and hooks.
They're in bags and in boxes and bureaus,
and pressed in the pages of books.

There are pretty ones sewn to the cushions
and tastefully pinned to the drapes.
The ceilings are coated with pancakes,
and the carpets are covered with crepes.

I have pancakes in most of my pockets,
and concealed in the linings of suits.
There are tiny ones stuffed in my mittens
and larger ones packed in my boots.

I have extras of most of my pancakes,
I maintain them in rows on these shelves,
and if you say nice things about them,
you may take a few home for yourselves.

I see that you've got to be going,
Won't you let yourselves out by the door?
It is time that I pour out the batter
and bake up a few hundred more.

The Frog Prince

Phoebe Hesketh

He was cold as slime,
Coloured to the underside
Of a rotted leaf
Mottled brown and yellow.

With promises of princehood underneath
The skin—if warmed by love—
He chose my pillow
For his transformation,
Croaked at me to stroke his throat
Pulsing like a swamp-bubble.

Pity froze to contempt;
Rather than touch him I lifted the pillow,
Flung him into the night.
Now alone in autumn mood I wonder
Who is this tall young man
Supple as willow and wind,
Carrying the sun on his shoulder.
His light shafts through me to its mark
In a girl not beautiful but kind.

Alice and the Frog

Brian Morse

Once upon a time
a princess called Alice
dropped her golden ball
in the ornamental pond
and a nameless frog
made her make a solemn promise
before doing
his big rescue act.

At tea-time
frog hopped gamely after,
rang the bell,
jumped between the major-domo's legs,
skittered down the marble hall,
forced his way past the footmen
and croaked his challenge.

Alice's father the king
knew at once what the frog was after
(the same had happened to his elder daughter).
Despite the princess's caterwauling
he accepted the amphibian
as his future son-in-law—
Prince of *Where-Did-You-Say?*

Ravenous, the frog supped keenly
and royally
on the take-away McDonald's.
The ice cream made him chilly
but the brandy went down well.
The king gazed with growing excitement at the atlas
and made him slop his pad print
on a clean sheet of headed paper.

Upstairs the frog pattered after Alice
puffed and panted into the bedroom
where the princess was taking off her make-up.
I suppose we better get this over,
she said, giving him a dry kiss,
then pushed him aside without a glance
to have a look at her bridal costume catalogue.

Downstairs Dad was packing
the royal jewels but not the debts.
You're sure Ruritania's sunny?
he said to the travel-agent
over the phone
before it was cut.
His title's good? They really have oil?
Yes, a single ticket.

Oh! and then the wedding
and the honeymoon.
Don't you wish you were here
the king's postcard says.
But Alice lies a-bed
(she nicked her finger)
the privet's growing thicker
and for the Prince
the footmen stand disconcertingly still.

A Spell for Midnight

Hal Summers

Yesterday is safe,
Tomorrow's full of danger,
Yesterday's a face I know,
Tomorrow is a stranger.

Tomorrow is a white sheet,
Yesterday's a written,
Tomorrow is for victory,
Yesterday is beaten.

Yesterday lies in a vault,
Tomorrow's on the move,
Yesterday's my money,
Tomorrow is my love.

Spell Against Sorrow

Kathleen Raine

Who will take away
Carry away sorrow,
Bear away grief?

Stream wash away
Float away sorrow,
Flow away, bear away
Wear away sorrow,
Carry away grief.

Mists hide away
Shroud my sorrow,
Cover the mountains,
Overcloud remembrance,
Hide away grief.

Earth take away
Make away sorrow,
Bury the lark's bones
Under the turf.
Bury my grief.

Black crow tear away
Rend away sorrow,
Talon and beak
Pluck out the heart
And the nerves of pain,
Tear away grief.

The Listeners

Walter de la Mare

'Is there anybody there?' said the Traveller,
  Knocking on the moonlit door;
And his horse in the silence champed the grasses
  Of the forest's ferny floor:
And a bird flew up out of the turret,
  Above the Traveller's head:
And he smote upon the door again a second time;
  'Is there anybody there?' he said.
But no one descended to the Traveller;
  No head from the leaf-fringed sill
Leaned over and looked into his grey eyes,
  Where he stood perplexed and still.
But only a host of phantom listeners
  That dwelt in the lone house then
Stood listening in the quiet of the moonlight
  To that voice from the world of men:
Stood thronging the faint moonbeams on the dark stair,
  That goes down to the empty hall,
Hearkening in an air stirred and shaken
  By the lonely Traveller's call.
And he felt in his heart their strangeness,
  Their stillness answering his cry,
While his horse moved, cropping the dark turf,
  'Neath the starred and leafy sky;
For he suddenly smote on the door, even
  Louder, and lifted his head:—
'Tell them I came, and no one answered,
  That I kept my word,' he said.

Never the least stir made the listeners,
    Though every word he spake
Fell echoing through the shadowiness of the still house
    From the one man left awake:
Ay, they heard his foot upon the stirrup,
    And the sound of iron on stone,
And how the silence surged softly backward,
    When the plunging hoofs were gone.

Welsh Incident

Robert Graves

'But that was nothing to what things came out
From the sea-caves of Criccieth yonder.'
'What were they? Mermaids? dragons? ghosts?'
'Nothing at all of any things like that.'
'What were they, then?'
                              'All sorts of queer things,
Things never seen or heard or written about,
Very strange, un-Welsh, utterly peculiar
Things. Oh, solid enough they seemed to touch,
Had anyone dared it. Marvellous creation,
All various shapes and sizes, and no sizes,
All new, each perfectly unlike his neighbour,
Though all came moving slowly out together.'
'Describe just one of them.'
                              'I am unable.'
'What were their colours?'
                              'Mostly nameless colours,
Colours you'd like to see; but one was puce
Or perhaps more like crimson, but not purplish.
Some had no colour.'
                              'Tell me, had they legs?'
'Not a leg nor foot among them that I saw.'
'But did these things come out in any order?
What o'clock was it? What was the day of the week?
Who else was present? How was the weather?'
'I was coming to that. It was half-past three
On Easter Tuesday last. The sun was shining.
The Harlech Silver Band played *Marchog Jesu*
On thirty-seven shimmering instruments,
Collecting for Caernarvon's (Fever) Hospital Fund.

The populations of Pwllheli, Criccieth,
Portmadoc, Borth, Tremadoc, Penrhyndeudraeth,
Were all assembled. Criccieth's mayor addressed them
First in good Welsh and then in fluent English,
Twisting his fingers in his chain of office,
Welcoming the things. They came out on the sand,
Not keeping time to the band, moving seaward
Silently at a snail's pace. But at last
The most odd, indescribable thing of all,
Which hardly one man there could see for wonder,
Did something recognizably a something.'
'Well, what?'
                    'It made a noise.'
                                        'A frightening noise?'
'No, no.'
            'A musical noise? A noise of scuffling?'
'No, but a very loud, respectable noise—
Like groaning to oneself on Sunday morning
In Chapel, close before the second psalm.'
'What did the mayor do?'
                                    'I was coming to that.'

Dialogue Between Ghost and Priest

Sylvia Plath

In the rectory garden on his evening walk
Paced brisk Father Shawn. A cold day, a sodden one it was
In black November. After a sliding rain
Dew stood in chill sweat on each stalk,
Each thorn; spiring from wet earth, a blue haze
Hung caught in dark-webbed branches like a fabulous heron.

Hauled sudden from solitude,
Hair prickling on his head,
Father Shawn perceived a ghost
Shaping itself from that mist.

'How now,' Father Shawn crisply addressed the ghost
Wavering there, gauze-edged, smelling of woodsmoke,
'What manner of business are you on?
From your blue pallor, I'd say you inhabited the frozen waste
Of hell, and not the fiery part. Yet to judge by that dazzled look,
That noble mien, perhaps you've late quitted heaven?'

In voice furred with frost,
Ghost said to priest:
'Neither of those countries do I frequent:
Earth is my haunt.'

'Come, come,' Father Shawn gave an impatient shrug,
'I don't ask you to spin some ridiculous fable
Of gilded harps or gnawing fire: simply tell
After your life's end, what just epilogue
God ordained to follow up your days. Is it such trouble
To satisfy the questions of a curious old fool?'

'In life, love gnawed my skin
To this white bone;
What love did then, love does now:
Gnaws me through.'

'What love,' asked Father Shawn, 'but too great love
Of flawed earth-flesh could cause this sorry pass?
Some damned condition you are in:
Thinking never to have left the world, you grieve
As though alive, shriveling in torment thus
To atone as shade for sin that lured blind man.'

'The day of doom
Is not yet come.
Until that time
A crock of dust is my dear home.'

'Fond phantom,' cried shocked Father Shawn,
'Can there be such stubbornness—
A soul grown feverish, clutching its dead body-tree
Like a last storm-crossed leaf? Best get you gone
To judgment in a higher court of grace.
Repent, depart, before God's trump-crack splits the sky.'

From that pale mist
Ghost swore to priest:
'There sits no higher court
Than man's red heart.'

Mary Celeste
Judith Nicholls

Only the wind sings
in the riggings,
the hull creaks a lullaby;
* a sail lifts gently*
*   like a message*
*   pinned to a vacant sky.*
*   The wheel turns*
*   over bare decks,*
*   shirts flap on a line;*
*   only the song of the lapping waves*
*   beats steady time ...*

First mate,
  off-duty from
    the long dawn watch, begins
      a letter to his wife, daydreams
      of home.

The Captain's wife is late;
  the child did not sleep
  and breakfast has passed ...
She, too, is missing home;
  sits down at last to eat,
  but can't quite force
  the porridge down.
  She swallows hard,
    slices the top from her egg.

The second mate
  is happy.
      A four-hour sleep,
  full stomach
and a quiet sea
are all he craves.

He has all three.

Shirts washed and hung, beds
made below, decks done, the boy
stitches a torn sail.

The Captain
has a good ear for a tune;
played his child to sleep
on the ship's organ.
Now, music left,
he checks his compass,
lightly tips the wheel,
hopes for a westerly.
Clear sky, a friendly sea,
fair winds for Italy.

The child now sleeps, at last,
head firmly pressed into her pillow
in a deep sea-dream.

Then why are the gulls wheeling
like vultures in the sky?
Why was the child snatched
from her sleep? What drew
the Captain's cry?

Only the wind replies
in the rigging,
and the hull creaks and sighs;
a sail spells out its message
over silent skies.
The wheel still turns
over bare decks,
shirts blow on the line;
the siren-song of lapping waves
still echoes over time.

Great Black-Backed Gulls

John Heath-Stubbs

Said Cap'n Morgan to Cap'n Kidd:
'Remember the grand times, Cap'n, when
The Jolly Roger flapped on the tropic breeze,
And we were the terrors of the Spanish Main?'
And Cap'n Kidd replied: 'Aye when our restless souls
Were steeped in human flesh and bone;
But now we range the seven seas, and fight
For galley scraps that men throw overboard.'

Two black-backed gulls, that perched
On a half-sunken spar—
Their eyes were gleaming cold and through
The morning fog that crept upon the grey-green waves
Their wicked laughter sounded.

They Call to One Another

George Barker

They call to one another
  in the prisons of the sea
the mermen and mermaidens
  bound under lock and key
down in the green and salty dens
  and dungeons of the sea,
lying about in chains but
  dying to be free:
and this is why shortsighted men
  believe them not to be
for down to their dark dungeons it
  is very hard to see.

But sometimes morning fishermen
  drag up in the net
bits of bright glass or the silver comb
  of an old vanity set
or a letter rather hard to read
  because it is still wet
sent to remind us never, never
  never to forget
the mermen and mermaidens
  in the prisons of the sea
who call to one another
  when the stars of morning rise
and the stars of evening set
  for I have heard them calling
and I can hear them, yet.

Everyone Sang

Siegfried Sassoon

Everyone suddenly burst out singing;
And I was filled with such delight
As prisoned birds must find in freedom,
Winging wildly across the white
Orchards and dark-green fields; on—on—and out
   of sight.

Everyone's voice was suddenly lifted;
And beauty came like the setting sun:
My heart was shaken with tears; and horror
Drifted away . . . O, but Everyone
Was a bird; and the song was wordless; the singing
   will never be done.

The Animals' Arrival

Elizabeth Jennings

So they came
Grubbing, rooting, barking, sniffing,
Feeling for cold stars, for stone, for some hiding-place,
Loosed at last from heredity, able to eat
From any tree or from ground, merely mildly themselves,
And every movement was quick, was purposeful, was proposed.
The galaxies gazed on, drawing in their distances.
The beasts breathed out warm on the air.

No one had come to make anything of this,
To move it, name it, shape it a symbol;
The huge creatures were their own depth, the hills
Lived lofty there, wanting no climber.
Murmur of birds came, rumble of underground beasts
And the otter swam deftly over the broad river.

There was silence too.
Plants grew in it, it wove itself, it spread, it enveloped
The evening as day-calls died and the universe hushed, hushed.
A last bird flew, a first beast swam
And prey on prey
Released each other
(Nobody hunted at all):
They slept for the waiting day.

The Tickle Rhyme
Ian Serraillier

'Who's that tickling my back?' said the wall.
'Me,' said a small
Caterpillar. 'I'm learning
To crawl.'

The Example
W. H. Davies

Here's an example from
   A Butterfly;
That on a rough, hard rock
   Happy can lie;
Friendless and all alone
On this unsweetened stone.

Now let my bed be hard,
   No care take I;
I'll make my joy like this
   Small Butterfly;
Whose happy heart has power
To make a stone a flower.

Considering the Snail

Thom Gunn

The snail pushes through a green
night, for the grass is heavy
with water and meets over
the bright path he makes, where rain
has darkened the earth's dark. He
moves in a wood of desire,

pale antlers barely stirring
as he hunts. I cannot tell
what power is at work, drenched there
with purpose, knowing nothing.
What is a snail's fury? All
I think is that if later

I parted the blades above
the tunnel and saw the thin
trail of broken white across
litter, I would never have
imagined the slow passion
to that deliberate progress.

The Sloth

Theodore Roethke

In moving-slow he has no Peer.
You ask him something in his ear;
He thinks about it for a Year;

And, then, before he says a Word
There, upside down (unlike a Bird)
He will assume that you have Heard—

A most Ex-as-per-at-ing Lug.
But should you call his manner Smug,
He'll sigh and give his Branch a Hug;

Then off again to Sleep he goes,
Still swaying gently by his Toes,
And you just *know* he knows he knows.

Something Told the Wild Geese

Rachel Field

Something told the wild geese
  It was time to go.
Though the fields lay golden
  Something whispered,—'Snow.'
Leaves were green and stirring,
  Berries, luster-glossed,

But beneath warm feathers
  Something cautioned,—'Frost.'
All the sagging orchards
  Steamed with amber spice,
But each wild breast stiffened
  At remembered ice.
Something told the wild geese
  It was time to fly,—
Summer sun was on their wings,
  Winter in their cry.

Don't Call Alligator Long-Mouth Till You Cross River

John Agard

Call alligator long-mouth
call alligator saw-mouth
call alligator pushy-mouth
call alligator scissors-mouth
call alligator raggedy-mouth
call alligator bumpy-bum
call alligator all dem rude word
but better wait
                till you cross river.

Trophy
(Thorpe Satchville Beagles, 3 hours,
Clawson, January 26th 1928)

Gillian Clarke

In the ice-trap of January
trees splinter a low sun
and the pond's brilliance
is glazed to pearl like the eye
of the old blind dog.

Hares start from furrows
to fire the land, their ears
small standing shadows, each bone
an instrument for listening,
each foot on the pulse of the earth.

Musk in the brain, the hounds
are a parliament of braying.
Of all creatures the hare
has the largest heart,
his blood-volume the greatest.

This one outran the pack
for a hare's nine lives,
and does again through an afternoon
when trees sing in ice, and air
is opal for three winter hours.

I heard of a hare who outran hounds
for a day and died of heartburst, found
at his death-moment, his arteries
full of air-bubbles instead of blood.

Or hares on aerodrome runways
racing the jets taking off.

When they cast the torn body away
and saved the golden head
for the taxidermist's shield,
in turn they emptied the horn
in the Star, Long Clawson.

At Thorpe Satchville the kennelman
set bowls before his pets,
and rubbed their coats
to their usual shining.

We are Going to See the Rabbit

Alan Brownjohn

We are going to see the rabbit,
We are going to see the rabbit.
Which rabbit, people say?
Which rabbit, ask the children?
Which rabbit?
The only rabbit,
The only rabbit in England,
Sitting behind a barbed-wire fence
Under the floodlights, neon lights,
Sodium lights,
Nibbling grass
On the only patch of grass
In England, in England
(Except the grass by the hoardings
Which doesn't count.)
We are going to see the rabbit
And we must be there on time.

First we shall go by escalator,
Then we shall go by underground,
And then we shall go by motorway
And then by helicopterway,
And the last ten yards we shall have to go
On foot.

And now we are going
All the way to see the rabbit,
We are nearly there,
We are longing to see it,
And so is the crowd
Which is here in thousands
With mounted policemen
And big loudspeakers
And bands and banners,
And everyone has come a long way.
But soon we shall see it
Sitting and nibbling
The blades of grass
On the only patch of grass
In—but something has gone wrong!
Why is everyone so angry,
Why is everyone jostling
And slanging and complaining?

The rabbit has gone,
Yes, the rabbit has gone.
He has actually burrowed down into the earth
And made himself a warren, under the earth,
Despite all these people.
And what shall we do?
What *can* we do?

It is all a pity, you must be disappointed,
Go home and do something else for today,
Go home again, go home for today.
For you cannot hear the rabbit, under the earth,
Remarking rather sadly to himself, by himself,
As he rests in his warren, under the earth:
'It won't be long, they are bound to come,
They are bound to come and find me, even here.'

Song of the Battery Hen

Edwin Brock

We can't grumble about accommodation:
we have a new concrete floor that's
always dry, four walls that are
painted white, and a sheet-iron roof
the rain drums on. A fan blows warm air
beneath our feet to disperse the smell
of chicken-shit and, on dull days,
fluorescent lighting sees us.

You can tell me: if you come by
the North door, I am in the twelfth pen
on the left-hand side of the third row
from the floor; and in that pen
I am usually the middle one of three.
But, even without directions, you'd
discover me. I have the same orange-
red comb, yellow beak and auburn
feathers, but as the door opens and you
hear above the electric fan a kind of
one-word wail, I am the one
who sounds loudest in my head.

Listen. Outside this house there's an
orchard with small moss-green apple
trees; beyond that, two fields of
cabbages; then, on the far side of
the road, a broiler house. Listen:
one cockerel grows out of there, as
tall and proud as the first hour of sun.
Sometimes I stop calling with the others
to listen, and wonder if he hears me.

The next time you come here, look for me.
Notice the way I sound inside my head.
God made us all quite differently,
and blessed us with this expensive home.

The Snare

James Stephens

I hear a sudden cry of pain!
   There is a rabbit in a snare:
Now I hear the cry again,
   But I cannot tell from where.

But I cannot tell from where
   He is calling out for aid;
Crying on the frightened air,
   Making everything afraid.

Making everything afraid,
   Wrinkling up his little face,
As he cries again for aid;
   And I cannot find the place!

And I cannot find the place
   Where his paw is in the snare;
Little one! Oh, little one!
   I am searching everywhere.

Cat's Funeral

E. V. Rieu

Bury her deep, down deep,
Safe in the earth's cold keep,
Bury her deep—

No more to watch bird stir;
No more to clean dark fur;
No more to glisten as silk;
No more to revel in milk;
No more to purr.

Bury her deep, down deep;
She is beyond warm sleep.
She will not walk in the night;
She will not wake to the light.
Bury her deep.

The Thought-Fox

Ted Hughes

I imagine this midnight moment's forest:
Something else is alive
Beside the clock's loneliness
And this blank page where my fingers move.

Through the window I see no star:
Something more near
Though deeper within darkness
Is entering the loneliness:

Cold, delicately as the dark snow,
A fox's nose touches twig, leaf;
Two eyes serve a movement, that now
And again now, and now, and now

Sets near prints into the snow
Between trees, and warily a lame
Shadow lags by stump and in hollow
Of a body that is bold to come

Across clearings, an eye,
A widening deepening greenness,
Brilliantly, concentratedly,
Coming about its own business

Till, with a sudden sharp hot stink of fox
It enters the dark hole of the head.
The window is starless still; the clock ticks,
The page is printed.

Dog Body and Cat Mind

Jenny Joseph

The dog body and cat mind
Lay in the room with the fire dying.
Will went out and locked the door.

Then the dog started howling.
He went to the door and scratched at it.
He went to the window and barked at it.
He prowled round the room sniffing and whining
Put his nose to the wainscot and whimpered in the dust.
The dog body and the cat mind
Locked in a room with the fire dying
And the dog would not lie down and be still.

He hurtled his shoulders against the wall;
He upset the cat's food and stepped in it.
He barked hard at his wild reflection
In the blank window. And banged his head
Until it ached, on the stone floor,
And still could not lie down and be still.

Then worn out with howling
And scratching and banging the dog flopped
To a weary defeated sleep.

And then the cat got up and started walking.

Poem

William Carlos Williams

As the cat
climbed over
the top of

the jamcloset
first the right
forefoot

carefully
then the hind
stepped down

into the pit of
the empty
flowerpot

Horses on the Camargue

Roy Campbell

In the grey wastes of dread,
The haunt of shattered gulls where nothing moves
But in a shroud of silence like the dead,
I heard a sudden harmony of hooves,
And, turning, saw afar
A hundred snowy horses unconfined,
The silver runaways of Neptune's car
Racing, spray curled, like waves before the wind.
Sons of the Mistral, fleet
As him with whose strong gusts they love to flee,
Who shod the flying thunders on their feet
And plumed them with the snortings of the sea;
Theirs is no earthly breed
Who only haunt the verges of the earth
And only on the sea's salt herbage feed—
Surely the great white breakers gave them birth.
For when for years a slave,
A horse of the Camargue, in alien lands,
Should catch some far-off fragrance of the wave
Carried far inland from his native sands,
Many have told the tale
Of how in fury, foaming at the rein,
He hurls his rider; and with lifted tail,
With coal-red eyes and cataracting mane,
Heading his course for home,
Though sixty foreign leagues before him sweep,
Will never rest until he breathes the foam
And hears the native thunder of the deep.

But when the great gusts rise
And lash their anger on these arid coasts,
When the scared gulls career with mournful cries
And whirl across the waste like driven ghosts:
When hail and fire converge,
The only souls to which they strike no pain
Are the white-crested fillies of the surge
And the white horses of the windy plain.
Then in their strength and pride
The stallions of the wilderness rejoice;
They feel their Master's trident in their side,
And high and shrill they answer to his voice.
With white tails smoking free,
Long streaming manes, and arching necks, they show
Their kinship to their sisters of the sea—
And forward hurl their thunderbolts of snow.
Still out of hardship bred,
Spirits of power and beauty and delight
Have ever on such frugal pastures fed
And loved to course with tempests through the night.

Horses

Edwin Muir

Those lumbering horses in the steady plough,
On the bare field—I wonder why, just now,
They seemed terrible, so wild and strange,
Like magic power on the stony grange.

Perhaps some childish hour has come again,
When I watched fearful, through the blackening rain,
Their hooves like pistons in an ancient mill
Move up and down, yet seem as standing still.

Their conquering hooves which trod the stubble down
Were ritual that turned the fields to brown,
And their great hulks were seraphim of gold
Or mute ecstatic monsters on the mould.

And oh the rapture, when, one furrow done,
They marched broad-breasted to the sinking sun!
The light flowed off their bossy sides in flakes;
The furrows rolled behind like struggling snakes.

But when at dusk with steaming nostrils home
They came, they seemed gigantic in the gloom,
And warm and glowing with mysterious fire
That lit their smouldering bodies in the mire.

Their eyes as brilliant and as wide as night
Gleamed with a cruel apocalyptic light.
Their manes the leaping ire of the wind
Lifted with rage invisible and blind.

Ah, now it fades! it fades! and I must pine
Again for that dread country crystalline,
Where the blank field and the still-standing tree
Were bright and fearful presences to me.

The Donkey

G. K. Chesterton

When fishes flew and forests walked
  And figs grew upon thorn,
Some moment when the moon was blood
  Then surely I was born;

With monstrous head and sickening cry
  And ears like errant wings,
The devil's walking parody
  On all four-footed things.

The tattered outlaw of the earth,
  Of ancient crooked will;
Starve, scourge, deride me: I am dumb,
  I keep my secret still.

Fools! For I also had my hour;
  One far fierce hour and sweet:
There was a shout about my ears,
  And palms before my feet.

Fetching Cows

Norman MacCaig

The black one, last as usual, swings her head
And coils a black tongue round a grass-tuft. I
Watch her soft weight come down, her split feet spread.

In front, the others swing and slouch; they roll
Their great Greek eyes and breathe out milky gusts
From muzzles black and shiny as wet coal.

The collie trots, bored, at my heels, then plops
Into the ditch. The sea makes a tired sound
That's always stopping though it never stops.

A haycart squats prick-eared against the sky.
Hay breath and milk breath. Far out in the west
The wrecked sun founders though its colours fly.

The collie's bored. There's nothing to control . . .
And the black cow is two native carriers
Bringing its belly home, slung from a pole.

The Flower-Fed Buffaloes

Vachel Lindsay

The flower-fed buffaloes of the spring
In the days of long ago,
Ranged where the locomotives sing
And the prairie flowers lie low:—
The tossing, blooming, perfumed grass
Is swept away by the wheat,
Wheels and wheels and wheels spin by
In the spring that still is sweet.
But the flower-fed buffaloes of the spring
Left us, long ago.
They gore no more, they bellow no more
They trundle around the hills no more:—
With the Blackfeet, lying low,
With the Pawnees, lying low,
Lying low.

Caring for Animals

Jon Silkin

I ask sometimes why these small animals
With bitter eyes, why we should care for them.

I question the sky, the serene blue water,
But it cannot say. It gives no answer.

And no answer releases in my head
A procession of grey shades patched and whimpering,

Dogs with clipped ears, wheezing cart horses
A fly without shadow and without thought.

Is it with these menaces to our vision
With this procession led by a man carrying wood

We must be concerned? The holy land, the rearing
Green island should be kindlier than this.

Yet the animals, our ghosts, need tending to.
Take in the whipped cat and the blinded owl;

Take up the man-trapped squirrel upon your shoulder.
Attend to the unnecessary beasts.

From growing mercy and a moderate love
Great love for the human animal occurs.

And your love grows. Your great love grows and grows.

CHILDHOOD

For a Five-year-old
Fleur Adcock

A snail is climbing up the window-sill
Into your room, after a night of rain.
You call me in to see, and I explain
That it would be unkind to leave it there:
It might crawl to the floor; we must take care
That no one squashes it. You understand,
And carry it outside, with careful hand,
To eat a daffodil.

I see, then, that a kind of faith prevails:
Your gentleness is moulded still by words
From me, who have trapped mice and shot wild birds,
From me, who drowned your kittens, who betrayed
Your closest relatives, and who purveyed
The harshest kind of truth to many another.
But that is how things are: I am your mother,
And we are kind to snails.

It Was Long Ago

Eleanor Farjeon

I'll tell you, shall I, something I remember?
Something that still means a great deal to me.
It was long ago.

A dusty road in summer I remember,
A mountain, and an old house, and a tree
That stood, you know,

Behind the house. An old woman I remember
In a red shawl with a grey cat on her knee
Humming under a tree.

She seemed the oldest thing I can remember,
But then perhaps I was not more than three.
It was long ago.

I dragged on the dusty road, and I remember
How the old woman looked over the fence at me
And seemed to know

How it felt to be three, and called out, I remember
'Do you like bilberries and cream for tea?'
I went under the tree

And while she hummed, and the cat purred, I remember
How she filled a saucer with berries and cream for me
So long ago,

Such berries and such cream as I remember
I never had seen before, and never see
Today, you know.

And that is almost all I can remember,
The house, the mountain, the grey cat on her knee,
Her red shawl, and the tree,

And the taste of the berries, the feel of the sun I remember,
And the smell of everything that used to be
So long ago,

Till the heat on the road outside again I remember,
And how the long dusty road seemed to have for me
No end, you know.

That is the farthest thing I can remember.
It won't mean much to you. It does to me.
Then I grew up, you see.

The Game of Life

Roy Fuller

Have you been in sight of heaven
Far ahead on ninety-seven,
Then swirled the dice and thrown a one,
Slid down a snake and flopped upon
Some square like sixty-three?

And then what made you even madder
Seen your sister climb a ladder
To eighty-four from twenty-eight
And felt a sudden rush of hate
As she smirked with glee?

And have you thought she counted out
(So as to miss a snake's dread snout)
A few too many squares—and stayed
Quiet because you were afraid
Or just through leniency?

If so, you will already know
How bitter life can be; and show
Upon your countenance no sign
Except perhaps a smile benign.
And shake on doggedly.

When I Was Christened
David McCord

When I was christened
they held me up
and poured some water
out of a cup.

The trouble was
it fell on me,
and I and water
don't agree.

A lot of christeners
stood and listened:
I let them know
that I was christened.

Adventures of Isabel

Ogden Nash

Isabel met an enormous bear,
Isabel, Isabel, didn't care;
The bear was hungry, the bear was ravenous,
The bear's big mouth was cruel and cavernous.
The bear said, Isabel, glad to meet you,
How do, Isabel, now I'll eat you!
Isabel, Isabel, didn't worry,
Isabel didn't scream or scurry.
She washed her hands and she straightened her hair up,
Then Isabel quietly ate the bear up.

Once in a night as black as pitch
Isabel met a wicked old witch.
The witch's face was cross and wrinkled,
The witch's gums with teeth were sprinkled.
Ho ho, Isabel! the old witch crowed,
I'll turn you into an ugly toad!
Isabel, Isabel, didn't worry,
Isabel didn't scream or scurry.
She showed no rage and she showed no rancor,
But she turned the witch into milk and drank her.

Isabel met a hideous giant,
Isabel continued self-reliant.
The giant was hairy, the giant was horrid,
He had one eye in the middle of his forehead.
Good morning, Isabel, the giant said,
I'll grind your bones to make my bread.
Isabel, Isabel, didn't worry,
Isabel didn't scream or scurry.
She nibbled the zwieback that she always fed off,
And when it was gone, she cut the giant's head off.

Isabel met a troublesome doctor,
He punched and he poked till he really shocked her.
The doctor's talk was of coughs and chills
And the doctor's satchel bulged with pills.
The doctor said unto Isabel,
Swallow this, it will make you well.
Isabel, Isabel, didn't worry,
Isabel didn't scream or scurry.
She took those pills from the pill concocter,
And Isabel calmly cured the doctor.

Father Says

Michael Rosen

Father says
Never
let
me
see
you
doing
that
again
father says
tell you once
tell you a thousand times
come hell or high water
his finger drills my shoulder
never let me see you doing that again

My brother knows all his phrases off by heart
so we practise them in bed at night.

Playgrounds
Berlie Doherty

Playgrounds are such gobby places.
Know what I mean?
Everyone seems to have something to
Talk about, giggle, whisper, scream and shout about.
I mean, it's like being in a parrot cage.

And playgrounds are such pushy places.
Know what I mean?
Everyone seems to have to
Run about, jump, kick, do cartwheels, handstands, fly around.
I mean, it's like being inside a whirlwind.

And playgrounds are such patchy places
Know what I mean?
Everyone seems to
Go round in circles, lines and triangles, coloured shapes,
I mean, it's like being in a kaleidoscope.

And playgrounds are such pally places
Know what I mean?
Everyone seems to
Have best friends, secrets, link arms, be in gangs.
Everyone, except me.

Know what I mean?

Where's Everybody?

Allan Ahlberg

In the cloakroom
Wet coats
Quietly steaming.

In the office
Dinner-money
Piled in pounds.

In the head's room
Half a cup
Of cooling tea.

In the corridor
Cupboards
But no crowds.

In the hall
Abandoned
Apparatus.

In the classrooms
Unread books
And unpushed pencils.

In the infants
Lonely hamster
Wendy house to let;

Deserted Plasticine
Still waters
Silent sand.

In the meantime
In the playground . . .
A fire-drill.

Truth

Barrie Wade

Sticks and stones may break my bones,
but words can also hurt me.
Stones and sticks break only skin,
while words are ghosts that haunt me.

Slant and curved the word-swords fall
to pierce and stick inside me.
Bats and bricks may ache through bones,
but words can mortify me.

Pain from words has left its scar
on mind and heart that's tender.
Cuts and bruises now have healed;
it's words that I remember.

Car Wash

Jackie Kay

Before it starts, she winds the window
up, fast enough to panic the glass.
A dramatic pause. Then the water
makes its loud music before
the big dancers begin their ballroom
spins. Done up to the nines,
in fancy red and yellow skirts.
We can't tell if they are
moving us or we are moving them.
Before we can say Tango or Rumba
they're on the roof, dancing a frantic
pas de bas pas de bas pas de bas.
My mum utters a manic
TWO THREE FOUR. We are about
to be swallowed up in their skirts.
All that terrible taffeta.
I go ga ga, shout Duck, Duck.
All of a sudden,
they just stop dancing.
Not even a feeble wee pas de double. Nothing.
Just stand back with their arms in the air.
Their hair full of electricity.
A green light flashes—GO—GO—
But we still haven't gone.
We've been here a week.
I go out to the station to get us odd
things to eat, but I've had it with Hulas
and barbecued beef. I want home.
My mum's actually clutching the wheel.
Says she's got no power in her elbow.
Doesn't like the look of the flashing—GO—
'Don't be daft, mother. Let's GO.'
'No, no, no,' she says, and turns on the radio.

The Tunnel

Brian Lee

This is the way that I have to go
I've left all my friends behind
Back there, where a faint light glimmers
Round the long tunnel's bend.

I can't see a roof up above me,
I can't find either wall,
My shoes slip on the slimy boulders—
How far is it down, if I fall?

Beneath me the same stream is flowing
That laughed in the fields back there—
Here, it is black, like the leeches and weeds,
And the bats flitting through the dank air.

It's just the same if I shut my eyes:
My companions, all around,
Are trickles, drips, sploshes, sudden *plops*,
Then, a strange, sucking sound.

One shoe's full of the cold dark water,
My hands slither over the stones,
My throat's gone dry, my heart pound-pounds,
But I can only go on—

Till I can see them, they can see me
And again they start to shout,
The rats bite, watch out for the rats,
But now I am almost out:

Dizzy, happy, I blink at the light,
The sun's still shining, the birds still sing.
Someone is patting me on the back—
Now I am one of the gang.

Tich Miller

Wendy Cope

Tich Miller wore glasses
with Elastoplast-pink frames
and had one foot three sizes larger than the other.

When they picked teams for outdoor games
she and I were always the last two
left standing by the wire-mesh fence.

We avoided one another's eyes,
stooping, perhaps, to re-tie a shoelace,
or affecting interest in the flight

of some fortunate bird, and pretended
not to hear the urgent conference:
'Have Tubby!' 'No, no, have Tich!'

Usually they chose me, the lesser dud,
and she lolloped, unselected,
to the back of the other team.

At eleven we went to different schools.
In time I learned to get my own back,
sneering at hockey-players who couldn't spell.

Tich died when she was twelve.

Televised

Maya Angelou

Televised news turns
a half-used day into
a waste of desolation.
If nothing wondrous preceded
the catastrophic announcements,
certainly nothing will follow, save
the sad-eyed faces of
bony children,
distended bellies making
mock at their starvation.
Why are they always
Black?
Whom do they await?
The lamb-chop flesh
reeks and cannot be
eaten. Even the
green peas roll on my plate
unmolested. Their innocence
matched by the helpless
hope in the children's faces.
Why do Black children
hope? Who will bring
them peas and lamb chops
and one more morning?

The Shoes

John Mole

These are the shoes
Dad walked about in
When we did jobs
In the garden,
When his shed
Was full of shavings,
When he tried
To put the fence up,
When my old bike
Needed mending,
When the car
Could not get started,
When he got up late
On Sunday.
These are the shoes
Dad walked about in
And I've kept them
In my room.

These are not the shoes
That Dad walked out in
When we didn't know
Where he was going,
When I tried to lift
His suitcase,
When he said goodbye
And kissed me,
When he left his door-key
On the table,
When he promised Mum
He'd send a postcard,
When I couldn't hear
His special footsteps.
These are not the shoes
That Dad walked out in
But he'll need them
When he comes back home.

Into My Heart

A. E. Housman

Into my heart an air that kills
    From yon far country blows:
What are those blue remembered hills,
    What spires, what farms are those?

That is the land of lost content,
    I see it shining plain,
The happy highways where I went
    And cannot come again.

Fern Hill

Dylan Thomas

Now as I was young and easy under the apple boughs
About the lilting house and happy as the grass was green,
   The night above the dingle starry,
      Time let me hail and climb
   Golden in the heydays of his eyes,
And honoured among wagons I was prince of the apple towns
And once below a time I lordly had the trees and leaves
      Trail with daisies and barley
   Down the rivers of the windfall light.

And as I was green and carefree, famous among the barns
About the happy yard and singing as the farm was home,
   In the sun that is young once only,
      Time let me play and be
   Golden in the mercy of his means,
And green and golden I was huntsman and herdsman, the calves
Sang to my horn, the foxes on the hills barked clear and cold,
      And the sabbath rang slowly
   In the pebbles of the holy streams.

All the sun long it was running, it was lovely, the hay
Fields high as the house, the tunes from the chimneys, it was air
   And playing, lovely and watery
      And fire green as grass.
   And nightly under the simple stars
As I rode to sleep the owls were bearing the farm away,
All the moon long I heard, blessed among stables, the night-jars
   Flying with the ricks, and the horses
      Flashing into the dark.

And then to awake, and the farm, like a wanderer white
With the dew, come back, the cock on his shoulder: it was all
   Shining, it was Adam and maiden,
      The sky gathered again
    And the sun grew round that very day
So it must have been after the birth of the simple light
In the first, spinning place, the spellbound horses walking warm
   Out of the whinnying green stable
    On to the fields of praise.

And honoured among foxes and pheasants by the gay house
Under the new made clouds and happy as the heart was long,
   In the sun born over and over,
    I ran my heedless ways,
    My wishes raced through the house high hay
And nothing I cared, at my sky blue trades, that time allows
In all his tuneful turning so few and such morning songs
   Before the children green and golden
    Follow him out of grace,

Nothing I cared, in the lamb white days, that time would take me
Up to the swallow thronged loft by the shadow of my hand,
   In the moon that is always rising.
    Nor that riding to sleep
   I should hear him fly with the high fields
And wake to the farm forever fled from the childless land.
Oh as I was young and easy in the mercy of his means,
    Time held me green and dying
   Though I sang in my chains like the sea.

By St Thomas Water

Charles Causley

By St Thomas Water
Where the river is thin
We looked for a jam-jar
To catch the quick fish in.
Through St Thomas Churchyard
Jessie and I ran
The day we took the jam-pot
Off the dead man.

On the scuffed tombstone
The grey flowers fell,
Cracked was the water,
Silent the shell.
The snake for an emblem
Swirled on the slab,
Across the beach of sky the sun
Crawled like a crab.

'If we walk,' said Jessie,
'Seven times round,
We shall hear a dead man
Speaking underground.'
Round the stone we danced, we sang,
Watched the sun drop,
Laid our heads and listened
At the tomb-top.

Soft as the thunder
At the storm's start
I heard a voice as clear as blood,
Strong as the heart.
But what words were spoken
I can never say,
I shut my fingers round my head,
Drove them away.

'What are those letters, Jessie,
Cut so sharp and trim
All round this holy stone
With earth up to the brim?'
Jessie traced the letters
Black as coffin-lead.
'*He is not dead but sleeping,*'
Slowly she said.

I looked at Jessie,
Jessie looked at me,
And our eyes in wonder
Grew wide as the sea.

Past the green and bending stones
We fled hand in hand,
Silent through the tongues of grass
To the river strand.

By the creaking cypress
We moved as soft as smoke
For fear all the people
Underneath awoke.
Over all the sleepers
We darted light as snow
In case they opened up their eyes,
Called us from below.

Many a day has faltered
Into many a year
Since the dead awoke and spoke
And we would not hear.
Waiting in the cold grass
Under a crinkled bough,
Quiet stone, cautious stone,
What do you tell me now?

I Wish I Were . . .

Rabindranath Tagore

When the gong sounds ten in the morning and I
walk to school by our lane,
Every day I meet the hawker crying, 'Bangles, crystal
bangles?'
There is nothing to hurry him on, there is no road he
must take, no place he must go to, no time when he
must come home.
I wish I were a hawker, spending my day in the road,
crying 'Bangles, crystal bangles!'
When at four in the afternoon I come back from the
school,
I can see through the gate of that house the gardener
digging the ground.
He does what he likes with his spade, he soils his clothes
with dust,
Nobody takes him to task if he gets baked in the sun or
gets wet.
I wish I were a gardener digging away at the garden
with nobody to stop me from digging.
Just as it gets dark in the evening and my mother sends
me to bed,
I can see through the open window the watchman
walking up and down.
The lane is dark and lonely, and the street-lamp stands
like a giant with one red eye in its head.
The watchman swings his lantern and walks with his
shadow at his side, and never once goes to bed in his
life.
I wish I were a watchman walking the streets all night,
chasing the shadows with my lantern.

Lost Days

Stephen Spender

Then, when an hour was twenty hours, he lay
Drowned under grass. He watched the carrier ant,
With mandibles as trolley, push in front
Wax-yellow specks across the parched cracked clay.
A tall sun made the stems down there transparent.
Moving, he saw the speedwell's sky blue eye
Start up next to his own, a chink of sky
Stamped deep through the tarpaulin of a tent.
He pressed his mouth against the rooted ground.
Held in his arms, he felt the earth spin round.

A Child's Calendar

George Mackay Brown

No visitors in January.
A snowman smokes a cold pipe in the yard.

They stand about like ancient women,
The February hills.
They have seen many a coming and going, the hills.

In March, Moorfea is littered
With knock-kneed lambs.

Daffodils at the door in April,
Three shawled Marys.
A lark splurges in galilees of sky.

And in May
Peatmen strike the bog with spades,
Summoning black fire.

The June bee
Bumps in the pane with a heavy bag of plunder.

Strangers swarm in July
With cameras, binoculars, bird books.

He thumped the crag in August,
A blind blue whale.

September crofts get wrecked in blond surges.
They struggle, the harvesters,
They drag loaf and ale-kirn into winter.

In October the fishmonger
Argues, pleads, threatens at the shore.

Nothing in November
But tinkers at the door, keening, with cans.

Some December midnight
Christ, Lord, lie warm in our byre.
Here are stars, an ox, poverty enough.

Revelation

Liz Lochhead

I remember once being shown the black bull
when a child at the farm for eggs and milk.
They called him Bob—as though perhaps
you could reduce a monster
with the charm of a friendly name.
At the threshold of his outhouse, someone
held my hand and let me peer inside.
At first, only black
and the hot reek of him. Then he was immense,
his edges merging with the darkness, just
a big bulk and a roar to be really scared of,
a trampling, and a clanking tense with the chain's jerk.
His eyes swivelled in the great wedge of his tossed head.
He roared his rage. His nostrils gaped.

And in the yard outside,
oblivious hens picked their way about.
The faint and rather festive tinkling
behind the mellow stone and hasp was all they knew
of that Black Mass, straining at his chains.
I had always half-known he existed—
this antidote and Anti-Christ his anarchy
threatening the eggs, well rounded, self-contained—
and the placidity of milk.

I ran, my pigtails thumping on my back in fear,
past the big boys in the farm lane
who pulled the wings from butterflies and
blew up frogs with straws.
Past throned hedge and harried nest,
scared of the eggs shattering—
only my small and shaking hand on the jug's rim
in case the milk should spill.

Unrecorded Speech

Anna Adams

She says 'How was you?' Kissing. 'Come on in,
I'm all of a muck-sweat, having a merry go-round;
you've caught me doing my work.'
She doesn't clean, but circumvents the dirt.
Chairs stand on tables—'All of a tizz-wozz.'
(Has that been spelt before?) 'A lick of paint,'
she says, propping her brush in turps,
'freshens things up a bit.' She paints the door
and skirting-boards; washes white window-veils.
Houses, bedsitters, flats, extend herself.
She makes the best of it, but likes a move;
it's like a change of dress, changing address.
I've lost count of the changes. 'Home at last!'
is said too often to be credible.
We'll write it on her tomb, or jar of ash,
unless she sees us out.
She says 'The poor old lady,' of someone
no older than herself.
'She's gone a bit—you know, dear—gone a bit
doo-lally. Poor old thing. It takes all sorts—'
From childhood she remembers sparkling frost,
and walking out in it in Christmas clothes—
a coat her mother made her—vivid mauve—
'so bright against the snow.'
'And of a Friday afternoon
the teacher read to us. That was the best.'
Stories have been essential food since then.
Peg's Paper, H. E. Bates, Hardy and all
except romances; 'that don't interest me.'
She fills her days 'somehow', since Hubby died,
but she has grown since then.

'All in a lifetime, dear,' she says of death.
Her words may be dead language soon;
that's why I write them down. They will be heard
'never no more', as she said at the birth
of my husband, her only child,
proving that double negatives mean 'No'.

A Recollection

Frances Cornford

My father's friend came once to tea.
He laughed and talked. He spoke to me.
But in another week they said
That friendly pink-faced man was dead.

'How sad . . .' they said, 'the best of men . . .'
So I said, too, 'How sad'; but then
Deep in my heart I thought, with pride,
'I know a person who has died'.

The Lesson

Edward Lucie-Smith

'Your father's gone,' my bald headmaster said.
His shiny dome and brown tobacco jar
Splintered at once in tears. It wasn't grief.
I cried for knowledge which was bitterer
Than any grief. For there and then I knew
That grief has uses—that a father dead
Could bind the bully's fist a week or two;
And then I cried for shame, then for relief.

I was a month past ten when I learnt this:
I still remember how the noise was stilled
In school-assembly when my grief came in.
Some goldfish in a bowl quietly sculled
Around their shining prison on its shelf.
They were indifferent. All the other eyes
Were turned towards me. Somewhere in myself
Pride, like a goldfish, flashed a sudden fin.

Follower

Seamus Heaney

My father worked with a horse-plough,
His shoulders globed like a full sail strung
Between the shafts and the furrow.
The horses strained at his clicking tongue.

An expert. He would set the wing
And fit the bright steel-pointed sock.
The sod rolled over without breaking.
At the headrig, with a single pluck

Of reins, the sweating team turned round
And back into the land. His eye
Narrowed and angled at the ground,
Mapping the furrow exactly.

I stumbled in his hob-nailed wake,
Fell sometimes on the polished sod;
Sometimes he rode me on his back
Dipping and rising to his plod.

I wanted to grow up and plough,
To close one eye, stiffen my arm.
All I ever did was follow
In his broad shadow round the farm.

I was a nuisance, tripping, falling,
Yapping always. But today
It is my father who keeps stumbling
Behind me, and will not go away.

The Icing Hand
Tony Harrison

That they lasted only till the next high tide
bothered me, not him whose labour was to make
sugar lattices demolished when the bride,
with help from her groom's hot hand, first cut the cake.

His icing hand, gritty with sandgrains, guides
my pen when I try shaping memories of him
and his eyes scan with mine those rising tides
neither father nor his son could hope to swim.

His eyes stayed dry while I, the kid, would weep
to watch the castle that had taken us all day
to build and deck decay, one wave-surge sweep
our winkle-stuccoed edifice away.

Remembrance like iced cake crumbs in the throat,
remembrance like windblown Blackpool brine
overfills the poem's shallow moat
and first, ebbing, salts, then, flowing, floods this line.

Piano

D. H. Lawrence

Softly, in the dusk, a woman is singing to me;
Taking me back down the vista of years, till I see
A child sitting under the piano, in the boom of the tingling strings
And pressing the small, poised feet of a mother who smiles as she sings.

In spite of myself, the insidious mastery of song
Betrays me back, till the heart of me weeps to belong
To the old Sunday evenings at home, with winter outside
And hymns in the cozy parlour, the tinkling piano our guide.

So now it is vain for the singer to burst into clamour
With the great black piano appassionato. The glamour
Of childish days is upon me, my manhood is cast
Down in the flood of remembrance, I weep like a child for the past.

About Friends

Brian Jones

The good thing about friends
is not having to finish sentences.

I sat a whole summer afternoon with my friend once
on a river bank, bashing heels on the baked mud
and watching the small chunks slide into the water
and listening to them—plop plop plop.
He said, 'I like the twigs when they . . . you know . . .
like that.' I said, 'There's that branch . . .'
We both said, 'Mmmm'. The river flowed and flowed
and there were lots of butterflies, that afternoon.

I first thought there was a sad thing about friends
when we met twenty years later.
We both talked hundreds of sentences,
taking care to finish all we said,
and explain it all very carefully,
as if we'd been discovered in places
we should not be, and were somehow ashamed.

I understood then what the river meant by flowing.

Legend
Judith Wright

The blacksmith's boy went out with a rifle
and a black dog running behind.
Cobwebs snatched at his feet,
rivers hindered him,
thorn branches caught at his eyes to make him blind
and the sky turned into an unlucky opal,
but he didn't mind,
I can break branches, I can swim rivers, I can stare out any
   spider I meet,
said he to his dog and his rifle.

The blacksmith's boy went over the paddocks
with his old black hat on his head.
Mountains jumped in his way,
rocks rolled down on him,
and the old crow cried, You'll soon be dead.
And the rain came down like mattocks.
But he only said
I can climb mountains, I can dodge rocks, I can shoot an
   old crow any day,
and he went on over the paddocks.

When he came to the end of the day the sun began falling.
Up came the night ready to swallow him,
like the barrel of the gun,
like an old black hat,
like a black dog hungry to follow him.
Then the pigeon, the magpie and the dove began wailing
and the grass lay down to billow him.
His rifle broke, his hat flew away and his dog was gone
and the sun was falling.

But in front of the night the rainbow stood on a mountain,
just as his heart foretold.
He ran like a hare,
he climbed like a fox;
he caught it in his hands, the colour and the cold—
like a bar of ice, like the column of a fountain,
like a ring of gold.
The pigeon, the magpie and the dove flew to stare,
And the grass stood up again on the mountain.

The blacksmith's boy hung the rainbow on his shoulder
instead of his broken gun.
Lizards ran out to see,
snakes made way for him,
and the rainbow shone as brightly as the sun.
All the world said, Nobody is braver, nobody is bolder,
Nobody else has done
anything to equal it. He went home as bold as he could be
with the swinging rainbow on his shoulder.

Walking Away
for Sean
C. *Day Lewis*

It is eighteen years ago, almost to the day—
A sunny day with the leaves just turning,
The touch-lines new-ruled—since I watched you play
Your first game of football, then, like a satellite
Wrenched from its orbit, go drifting away

Behind a scatter of boys. I can see
You walking away from me towards the school
With the pathos of a half-fledged thing set free
Into a wilderness, the gait of one
Who finds no path where the path should be.

That hesitant figure, eddying away
Like a winged seed loosened from its parent stem
Has something I never quite grasp to convey
About nature's give-and-take—the small, the scorching
Ordeals which fire one's irresolute clay.

I have had worse partings, but none that so
Gnaws at my mind still. Perhaps it is roughly
Saying what God alone could perfectly show—
How selfhood begins with a walking away,
And love is proved in the letting go.

PEOPLE

The Leader
Roger McGough

I wanna be the leader
I wanna be the leader
Can I be the leader?
Can I? I can?
Promise? Promise?
Yippee, I'm the leader
I'm the leader

OK what shall we do?

The First Men on Mercury

Edwin Morgan

—We come in peace from the third planet.
Would you take us to your leader?

—Bawr stretter! Bawr. Bawr. Stretterhawl?

—This is a little plastic model
of the solar system, with working parts.
You are here and we are there and we
are now here with you, is this clear?

—Gawl horrop. Bawr. Abawrhannahanna!

—Where we come from is blue and white
with brown, you see we call the brown
here 'land', the blue is 'sea', and the white
is 'clouds' over land and sea, we live
on the surface of the brown land,
all round is sea and clouds. We are 'men'.
Men come—

—Glawp men! Gawrbenner menko. Menhawl?

—Men come in peace from the third planet
which we call 'earth'. We are earthmen.
Take us earthmen to your leader.

—Thmen? Thmen? Bawr. Bawrhossop.
Yuleeda tan hanna. Harrabost yuleeda.

—I am the yuleeda. You see my hands,
we carry no benner, we come in peace.
The spaceways are all stretterhawn.

—Glawn peacemen all horrabhanna tantko!
Tan come at'mstrossop. Glawp yuleeda!

—Atoms are peacegawl in our harraban.
Menbat worrabost from tan hannahanna.

—You men we know bawrhossoptant. Bawr.
We know yuleeda. Go strawg backspetter quick.

—We cantantabawr, tantingko backspetter now!

—Banghapper now! Yes, third planet back.
Yuleeda will go back blue, white, brown
nowhanna! There is no more talk.

—Gawl han fasthapper?

—No. You must go back to your planet.
Go back in peace, take what you have gained
but quickly.

—Stretterworra gawl, gawl . . .

—Of course, but nothing is ever the same,
now is it? You'll remember Mercury.

Resurrected

Matthew Sweeney

If I got out of my grave
in a hundred years' time
I'd ignore the other risen dead
sniffing flowers, brushing their clothes,
fixing their hair, feeling their faces—
I wouldn't even read my epitaph,
but I'd make for the river
and I'd jump in, with all my clothes on,
and I'd swim, stiffly, till I was clean,
then I'd climb on the boat
waiting to take us to town.
I'd speak to nobody,
as I'd have lost the habit,
and the language would have grown.
The later dead would stare at me,
at my once-again-trendy clothes,
and of course I'd be young again
with half an eye for the women,
but first I'd head for a bar
for a long-postponed beer, and I'd
ask where a Thai restaurant was,
shining my antique coins.

Pitying Heaven

Michael Baldwin

Mr McTaggart, good McTaggart,
   nice clean house-trained McTaggart
With his cool moist nose
   and glistening moustache
Wears a lead to his neck and a spiked collar.

On it a plate says
THE PROPERTY OF MRS McTAGGART,
15 The Pines, *please return*
   or ring 7373 we'll send round a basket

And the lead is attached
   to the ingenious, twenty-two carat fingers
Of the said Mrs McTaggart

Who is scared he'll slip off with the other dirty dogs
And be lost in the cat-filled dark.

About His Person
Simon Armitage

Five pounds fifty in change, exactly,
a library card on its date of expiry.

A postcard, stamped,
unwritten, but franked,

a pocket-size diary slashed with a pencil
from March twenty-fourth to the first of April.

A brace of keys for a mortise lock,
an analogue watch, self-winding, stopped.

A final demand
in his own hand,

a rolled-up note of explanation
planted there like a spray carnation

but beheaded, in his fist.
A shopping list.

A giveaway photograph stashed in his wallet,
a keepsake banked in the heart of a locket.

No gold or silver,
but crowning one finger

a ring of white unweathered skin.
That was everything.

Men of Terry Street

Douglas Dunn

They come in at night, leave in the early morning.
I hear their footsteps, the ticking of bicycle chains,
Sudden blasts of motorcycles, whimpering of vans.
Somehow I am either in bed, or the curtains are drawn.

This masculine invisibility makes gods of them,
A pantheon of boots and overalls.
But when you see them, home early from work
Or at their Sunday leisure, they are too tired

And bored to look long at comfortably.
It hurts to see their faces, too sad or too jovial.
They quicken their step at the smell of cooking,
They hold up their children and sing to them.

Every Day in Every Way
(Dr Coué: Every day in every way I grow
better and better)
Kit Wright

When I got up this morning
I thought the whole thing through:
Thought, Who's the hero, the man of the
day?
Christopher, it's you.

With my left arm I raised my right arm
High above my head:
Said, Christopher, you're the greatest.
Then I went back to bed.

I wrapped my arms around me,
No use counting sheep.
I counted legions of myself
Walking on the deep.

The sun blazed on the miracle,
The blue ocean smiled:
We like the way you operate,
Frankly, we like your style.

Dreamed I was in a meadow,
Angels singing hymns,
Fighting the nymphs and shepherds
Off my holy limbs.

A girl leaned out with an apple,
Said, You can taste for free.
I never touch the stuff, dear,

I'm keeping myself for me.

Dreamed I was in heaven,
God said, Over to you,
Christopher, you're the greatest!
And Oh, it's true, it's true!

I like my face in the mirror,
I like my voice when I sing.
My girl says it's just infatuation—
I know it's the real thing.

The Embankment
(The Fantasia of a Fallen Gentleman on a Cold, Bitter Night)

T. E. Hulme

Once, in finesse of fiddles found I ecstasy,
In a flash of gold heels on the hard pavement.
Now see I
That warmth's the very stuff of poesy.
Oh, God, make small
The old star-eaten blanket of the sky,
That I may fold it round me and in comfort lie.

The Man on the Desert Island (1)

Gerda Mayer

The man on the desert island
Has forgotten the ways of people,
His stories are all of himself.
Day in, day out of time,
He communes with himself and sends
Messages in green bottles:
Help me they say *I am*
Cast up and far from home.
Each day he goes to watch
The horizon for ships.
Nothing reaches his shore
Except corked green bottles.

Not Waving but Drowning

Stevie Smith

Nobody heard him, the dead man,
But still he lay moaning:
I was much further out than you thought
And not waving but drowning.

Poor chap, he always loved larking
And now he's dead.
It must have been too cold for him his heart gave way,
They said.

Oh, no no no, it was too cold always
(Still the dead one lay moaning)
I was much too far out all my life
And not waving but drowning.

Why Brownlee Left

Paul Muldoon

Why Brownlee left, and where he went,
Is a mystery even now.
For if a man should have been content
It was him; two acres of barley,
One of potatoes, four bullocks,
A milker, a slated farmhouse.
He was last seen going out to plough
On a March morning, bright and early.

By noon Brownlee was famous;
They had found all abandoned, with
The last rig unbroken, his pair of black
Horses, like man and wife,
Shifting their weight from foot to
Foot, and gazing into the future.

Hunger

Laurence Binyon

I come among the peoples like a shadow.
I sit down by each man's side.

None sees me, but they look on one another,
And know that I am there.

My silence is like the silence of the tide
That buries the playground of children;

Like the deepening of frost in the slow night,
When birds are dead in the morning.

Armies trample, invade, destroy,
With guns roaring from earth and air.

I am more terrible than armies,
I am more feared than cannon.

Kings and chancellors give commands;
I give no command to any;

But I am listened to more than kings
And more than passionate orators.

I unswear words, and undo deeds.
Naked things know me.

I am first and last to be felt of the living;
I am Hunger.

O What is That Sound

W. H. Auden

O what is that sound which so thrills the ear
  Down in the valley, drumming, drumming?
Only the scarlet soldiers, dear,
  The soldiers coming.

O what is that light I see flashing so clear
  Over the distance brightly, brightly?
Only the sun on their weapons, dear,
  As they step lightly.

O what are they doing with all that gear,
  What are they doing this morning, this morning?
Only their usual manoeuvres, dear,
  Or perhaps a warning.

O why have they left the road down there,
  Why are they suddenly wheeling, wheeling?
Perhaps a change in their orders, dear.
  Why are you kneeling?

O haven't they stopped for the doctor's care,
  Haven't they reined their horses, their horses?
Why, they are none of them wounded, dear,
  None of these forces.

O is it the parson they want, with white hair,
  Is it the parson, is it, is it?
No, they are passing his gateway, dear,
  Without a visit.

O it must be the farmer who lives so near.
  It must be the farmer so cunning, so cunning?
They have passed the farmyard already, dear,
  And now they are running.

O where are you going? Stay with me here!
   Were the vows you swore deceiving, deceiving?
No, I promised to love you, dear,
   But I must be leaving.

O it's broken the lock and splintered the door,
   O it's the gate where they're turning, turning;
Their boots are heavy on the floor
   And their eyes are burning.

Evans

R. S. Thomas

Evans? Yes, many a time
I came down his bare flight
Of stairs into the gaunt kitchen
With its wood fire, where crickets sang
Accompaniment to the black kettle's
Whine, and so into the cold
Dark to smother in the thick tide
Of night that drifted about the walls
Of his stark farm on the hill ridge.

It was not the dark filling my eyes
And mouth appalled me; not even the drip
Of rain like blood from the one tree
Weather-tortured. It was the dark
Silting the veins of that sick man
I left stranded upon the vast
And lonely shore of his bleak bed.

Not My Best Side

(*Uccello*: St George and the Dragon, *The National Gallery*)

U. A. Fanthorpe

I
Not my best side, I'm afraid.
The artist didn't give me a chance to
Pose properly, and as you can see,
Poor chap, he had this obsession with
Triangles, so he left off two of my
Feet. I didn't comment at the time
(What, after all, are two feet
To a monster?) but afterwards
I was sorry for the bad publicity.
Why, I said to myself, should my conqueror
Be so ostentatiously beardless, and ride
A horse with a deformed neck and square hoofs?
Why should my victim be so
Unattractive as to be inedible,
And why should she have me literally
On a string? I don't mind dying
Ritually, since I always rise again,
But I should have liked a little more blood
To show they were taking me seriously.

II
It's hard for a girl to be sure if
She wants to be rescued. I mean, I quite
Took to the dragon. It's nice to be
Liked, if you know what I mean. He was
So nicely physical, with his claws
And lovely green skin, and that sexy tail,
And the way he looked at me,
He made me feel he was all ready to
Eat me. And any girl enjoys that.

So when this boy turned up, wearing machinery,
On a really *dangerous* horse, to be honest,
I didn't much fancy him. I mean,
What was he like underneath the hardware?
He might have acne, blackheads or even
Bad breath for all I could tell, but the dragon—
Well, you could see all his equipment
At a glance. Still, what could I do?
The dragon got himself beaten by the boy,
And a girl's got to think of her future.

III
I have diplomas in Dragon
Management and Virgin Reclamation.
My horse is the latest model, with
Automatic transmission and built-in
Obsolescence. My spear is custom-built,
And my prototype armour
Still on the secret list. You can't
Do better than me at the moment.
I'm qualified and equipped to the
Eyebrow. So why be difficult?
Don't you want to be killed and/or rescued
In the most contemporary way? Don't
You want to carry out the roles
That sociology and myth have designed for you?
Don't you realize that, by being choosy,
You are endangering job-prospects
In the spear- and horse-building industries?
What, in any case, does it matter what
You want? You're in my way.

Old Woman

Iain Crichton Smith

And she, being old, fed from a mashed plate
as an old mare might droop across a fence
to the dull pastures of its ignorance.
Her husband held her upright while he prayed

to God who is all-forgiving to send down
some angel somewhere who might land perhaps
in his foreign wings among the gradual crops.
She munched, half dead, blindly searching the spoon.

Outside, the grass was raging. There I sat
imprisoned in my pity and my shame
that men and women having suffered time
should sit in such a place, in such a state

and wished to be away, yes, to be far away
with athletes, heroes, Greeks or Roman men
who pushed their bitter spears into a vein
and would not spend an hour with such decay.

'Pray God,' he said, 'we ask you, God,' he said.
The bowed back was quiet. I saw the teeth
tighten their grip around a delicate death.
And nothing moved within the knotted head

but only a few poor veins as one might see
vague wishless seaweed floating on a tide
of all the salty waters where had died
too many waves to mark two more or three.

Sensitive, Seldom, and Sad
Mervyn Peake

Sensitive, Seldom, and Sad are we,
As we wend our way to the sneezing sea,
With our hampers full of thistles and fronds
To plant round the edge of the dab-fish ponds;
Oh, so Sensitive, Seldom, and Sad—
Oh, *so* Seldom and Sad.

In the shambling shades of the shelving shore,
We will sing us a song of the Long Before,
And light a red fire and warm our paws
For it's chilly, it is, on the Desolate shores,
For those who are Sensitive, Seldom, and Sad.
For those who are Seldom and Sad.

Sensitive, Seldom, and Sad we are,
As we wander along through Lands Afar,
To the sneezing sea, where the sea-weeds be,
And the dab-fish ponds that are waiting for we
Who are, Oh, so Sensitive, Seldom, and Sad,
Oh, *so* Seldom and Sad.

The Doomed Spaceman

Ted Walker

I remember one winter-night meadow
Of sky-black grass
That lay beyond my childhood window
Of pearly glass
When I learned what it was to be lonely,
Packed off to bed
And lit by a glimmer that wanly
The frostfall shed.

The pane wiped clear, my crying over,
Darkness would yield
Its long cluster of summer-white clover
In a vast field;
Sleepless I stared for yearning hours,
And I began
Wanting to wander those infinite flowers
When a grown man.

And now I am lost in the heavens.
My meanderings
Further immeasurably flung than Saturn's
Exquisite rings
Into space that's unutterably lovely
With misted light
And every dusk is a dawn and every
Day is as night.

Straight my broken instruments steer:
I have no choice
But to bear silence in which I can hear
No human voice
Save mine at the capsule's clear window
When galaxies pass—
No dandelion Sun in no meadow
Of day-blue grass.

Weightless, helpless, I'm locked on a track
I can't reverse;
For one glimpse of home, I would give back
The universe.
Constellation by constellation
Like baby's breath
I journey through, my destination
Nowhere but Death.

A Martian Sends a Postcard Home

Craig Raine

Caxtons are mechanical birds with many wings
and some are treasured for their markings—

they cause the eyes to melt
or the body to shriek without pain.

I have never seen one fly, but
sometimes they perch on the hand.

Mist is when the sky is tired of flight
and rests its soft machine on ground:

then the world is dim and bookish
like engravings under tissue paper.

Rain is when the earth is television.
It has the property of making colours darker.

Model T is a room with the lock inside—
a key is turned to free the world

for movement, so quick there is a film
to watch for anything missed.

But time is tied to the wrist
or kept in a box, ticking with impatience.

In homes, a haunted apparatus sleeps,
that snores when you pick it up.

If the ghost cries, they carry it
to their lips and soothe it to sleep

with sounds. And yet, they wake it up
deliberately, by tickling with a finger.

Only the young are allowed to suffer
openly. Adults go to a punishment room

with water but nothing to eat.
They lock the door and suffer the noises

alone. No one is exempt
and everyone's pain has a different smell.

At night, when all the colours die,
they hide in pairs

and read about themselves—
in colour, with their eyelids shut.

SCENES

For the Record
Libby Houston

glancing away

saw for a second
neck and neck with us
on the motorway
some vole
going like one fur
cylinder—

no chance!

falling back fast
pulled out of it
shot off for its
own slow lane
through the briar—
like a star

in Just-spring
E. E. Cummings

in Just-
spring   when the world is mud-
luscious the little
lame balloonman

whistles   far   and wee

and eddieandbill come
running from marbles and
piracies and it's
spring

when the world is puddle-wonderful

the queer
old balloonman whistles
far   and   wee
and bettyandisbel come dancing

from hop-scotch and jump-rope and

it's
spring
and
      the

            goat-footed

balloonMan   whistles
far
and
wee

April Rain Song

Langston Hughes

Let the rain kiss you.
Let the rain beat upon your head with silver liquid drops.
Let the rain sing you a lullaby.

The rain makes still pools on the sidewalk.
The rain makes running pools in the gutter.
The rain plays a little sleep-song on our roof at night—

And I love the rain.

'There Will Come Soft Rains'

Sara Teasdale

There will come soft rains and the smell of the ground,
And swallows calling with their shimmering sound;

And frogs in the pools singing at night,
And wild-plum trees in tremulous white;

Robins will wear their feathery fire
Whistling their whims on a low fence-wire;

And not one will know of the war, not one
Will care at last when it is done.

Not one would mind, neither bird nor tree,
If mankind perished utterly;

And Spring herself, when she woke at dawn,
Would scarcely know that we were gone.

Day of These Days
Laurie Lee

Such a morning it is when love
leans through geranium windows
and calls with a cockerel's tongue.

When red-haired girls scamper like roses
over the rain-green grass,
and the sun drips honey.

When hedgerows grow venerable,
berries dry black as blood,
and holes suck in their bees.

Such a morning it is when mice
run whispering from the church,
dragging dropped ears of harvest.

When the partridge draws back his spring
and shoots like a buzzing arrow
over grained and mahogany fields.

When no table is bare,
and no breast dry,
and the tramp feeds off ribs of rabbit.

Such a day it is when time
piles up the hills like pumpkins,
and the streams run golden.

When all men smell good,
and the cheeks of girls
are as baked bread to the mouth.

As bread and beanflowers
the touch of their lips,
and their white teeth sweeter than cucumbers.

Midsummer, Tobago

Derek Walcott

Broad sun-stoned beaches.

White heat.
A green river.

A bridge,
scorched yellow palms

from the summer-sleeping house
drowsing through August.

Days I have held,
days I have lost,

days that outgrow, like daughters,
my harbouring arms.

Hard Frost

Andrew Young

Frost called to water 'Halt!'
And crusted the moist snow with sparkling salt;
Brooks, their own bridges, stop,
And icicles in long stalactites drop,
And tench in water-holes
Lurk under gluey glass like fish in bowls.

In the hard-rutted lane
At every footstep breaks a brittle pain,
And tinkling trees ice-bound,
Changed into weeping willows, sweep the ground;
Dead boughs take root in ponds
And ferns on windows shoot their ghostly fronds.

But vainly the fierce frost
Interns poor fish, ranks trees in an armed host,
Hangs daggers from house-eaves
And on the windows ferny ambush weaves;
In the long war grown warmer
The sun will strike him dead and strip his armour.

The Midnight Skaters

Edmund Blunden

The hop-poles stand in cones,
    The icy pond lurks under,
The pole-tops steeple to the thrones
    Of stars, sound gulfs of wonder;
But not the tallest there, 'tis said,
Could fathom to this pond's black bed.

Then is not death at watch
    Within those secret waters?
What wants he but to catch
    Earth's heedless sons and daughters?
With but a crystal parapet
Between, he has his engines set.

Then on, blood shouts, on, on,
    Twirl, wheel and whip above him,
Dance on this ball-floor thin and wan,
    Use him as though you love him;
Court him, elude him, reel and pass,
And let him hate you through the glass.

Fog
Carl Sandburg

The fog comes
on little cat feet.
It sits looking
over harbor and city
on silent haunches
and then moves on.

The More It Snows
A. A. Milne

The more it
SNOWS-tiddely-pom,
The more it
GOES-tiddely-pom,
The more it
GOES-tiddely-pom,
On
Snowing.

And nobody
KNOWS-tiddely-pom,
How cold my
TOES-tiddely-pom,
How cold my
TOES-tiddely-pom,
Are
Growing.

On a Night of Snow

Elizabeth Coatsworth

Cat, if you go outdoors, you must walk in the snow.
You will come back with little white shoes on your feet,
little white shoes of snow that have heels of sleet.
Stay by the fire, my Cat. Lie still, do not go.
See how the flames are leaping and hissing low,
I will bring you a saucer of milk like a marguerite,
so white and so smooth, so spherical and so sweet—
stay with me, Cat. Outdoors the wild winds blow.

Outdoors the wild winds blow, Mistress, and dark is the night,
strange voices cry in the trees, intoning strange lore,
and more than cats move, lit by our eyes' green light,
on silent feet where the meadow grasses hang hoar—
Mistress, there are portents abroad of magic and might,
and things that are yet to be done. Open the door!

London Snow

Robert Bridges

When men were all asleep the snow came flying,
In large white flakes falling on the city brown,
Stealthily and perpetually settling and loosely lying,
    Hushing the latest traffic of the drowsy town;
Deadening, muffling, stifling its murmurs failing;
Lazily and incessantly floating down and down:
    Silently sifting and veiling road, roof, and railing;
Hiding difference, making unevenness even,
Into angles and crevices softly drifting and sailing.
    All night it fell, and when full inches seven
It lay in the depth of its uncompacted lightness,
The clouds blew off from a high and frosty heaven;
    And all woke earlier for the unaccustomed brightness
Of the winter dawning, the strange unheavenly glare:
The eye marvelled—marvelled at the dazzling whiteness;
    The ear hearkened to the stillness of the solemn air;
No sound of wheel rumbling nor of foot falling,
And the busy morning cries came thin and spare.
    Then boys I heard, as they went to school, calling,
They gathered up the crystal manna to freeze
Their tongues with tasting, their hands with snowballing;
    Or rioted in a drift, plunging up to the knees;
Or peering up from under the white-mossed wonder,
'O look at the trees!' they cried. 'O look at the trees!'
    With lessened load a few carts creak and blunder,
Following along the white deserted way,
A country company long dispersed asunder:
    When now already the sun, in pale display
Standing by Paul's high dome, spread forth below
His sparkling beams, and awoke the stir of the day.

For now doors open, and war is waged with the snow;
And trains of sombre men, past tale of number,
Tread long brown paths, as toward their toil they go:
    But even for them awhile no cares encumber
Their minds diverted; the daily word is unspoken,
The daily thoughts of labour and sorrow slumber
At the sight of the beauty that greets them, for the charm they have broken.

When Skies are Low
and Days are Dark

N. M. Bodecker

When skies are low
and days are dark,
and frost bites
like a hungry shark,
when mufflers muffle
ears and nose,
and puffy sparrows
huddle close—
how nice to know
that February
is something purely
temporary.

The Side Way Back

Philip Gross

You're late. Take a chance up the cul-de-sac,
a short cut home. It's the side way back—
the way they tell you not to go,
the way the kids and stray cats know
as Lovebite Alley, Dead Dog Lane . . .
The Council says it's got no name.
                    All the same . . .

There's sharkstooth glass on a breezeblock wall.
There's nobody near to hear if you call.
There are tetanus tips on the rusty wire.
There's a house they bricked up after the fire
spraycanned with blunt names and a thinks-balloon
full of four-letter words and a grinning moon-
                    cartoon.

It's a narrow and narrowing one way street
down to the end where the night kids meet.
You've seen the scuffed-out tips of their fags.
You've smelt something wrong in their polythene bags.
There's a snuffle and a scratching at a planked-up gate.
There's a footstep you don't hear till almost too late.
                    Don't wait.

Now you're off and you're running for years and years
with the hissing of panic like rain in your ears.
You could run till you're old, you could run till you're gone
and never get home. To slow down and walk on
is hard. Harder still is to turn
and look back. Though it's slow as a Chinese burn,
                    you'll learn.

Southbound on the Freeway

May Swenson

A tourist came in from Orbitville,
parked in the air, and said:

The creatures of this star
are made of metal and glass.

Through the transparent parts
you can see their guts.

Their feet are round and roll
on diagrams—or long

measuring tapes—dark
with white lines.

They have four eyes.
The two in the back are red.

Sometimes you can see a five-eyed
one, with a red eye turning

on the top of his head.
He must be special—

the others respect him,
and go slow,

when he passes, winding
among them from behind.

They all hiss as they glide,
like inches, down the marked

tapes. Those soft shapes,
shadowy inside

the hard bodies—are they
their guts or their brains?

The Day the World Ended
for John Betjeman

George MacBeth

The washing machine was whirling away,
   The cat was licking its tail,
A pile of clothes was on top and done,
   And a pile was below in a pail.

The basement was growing steamy and warm,
   The cat was alert and wise,
The dryer was doing its job quite well,
   And the jeans were rattling their flies.

The regular wash was all clean and dry,
   The *Tide* was back on the sink,
The handkerchiefs were all fresh and smooth,
   And the towels looked bright and pink.

The revolving drum had come to a halt,
   The shirts were all shut inside,
The air was thick with the smell of suds,
   And the cat's eyes were open wide.

The world was travelling round the sun,
  The moon was out in the west,
A spider was tottering over the floor,
  And the maid was wringing a vest.

The hangers were on the clothes horse,
  The socks were dripping and wet,
The cat had gone for a plate of fish,
  And the sun had started to set.

The light was up in the living-room,
  The lamp was down in the hall,
The cat was hunting a brown rat,
  And nothing had happened at all.

Preludes

T. S. Eliot

I
The winter evening settles down
With smell of steaks in passageways.
Six o'clock.
The burnt-out ends of smoky days.
And now a gusty shower wraps
The grimy scraps
Of withered leaves about your feet
And newspapers from vacant lots;
The showers beat
On broken blinds and chimney-pots,
And at the corner of the street
A lonely cab-horse steams and stamps.

And then the lighting of the lamps.

II
The morning comes to consciousness
Of faint stale smells of beer
From the sawdust-trampled street
With all its muddy feet that press
To early coffee-stands.
With the other masquerades
That time resumes,
One thinks of all the hands
That are raising dingy shades
In a thousand furnished rooms.

III

You tossed a blanket from the bed,
You lay upon your back, and waited;
You dozed, and watched the night revealing
The thousand sordid images
Of which your soul was constituted;
They flickered against the ceiling.
And when all the world came back
And the light crept up between the shutters
And you heard the sparrows in the gutters,
You had such a vision of the street
As the street hardly understands;
Sitting along the bed's edge, where
You curled the papers from your hair,
Or clasped the yellow soles of feet
In the palms of both soiled hands.

IV

His soul stretched tight across the skies
That fade behind a city block,
Or trampled by insistent feet
At four and five and six o'clock;
And short square fingers stuffing pipes,
And evening newspapers, and eyes
Assured of certain certainties,
The conscience of a blackened street
Impatient to assume the world.
I am moved by fancies that are curled
Around these images, and cling:
The notion of some infinitely gentle
Infinitely suffering thing.

Wipe your hand across your mouth, and laugh;
The worlds revolve like ancient women
Gathering fuel in vacant lots.

Encounter at St Martin's

Ken Smith

I tell a wanderer's tale, the same
I began long ago, a boy in a barn,
I am always lost in it. The place
is always strange to me. In my pocket

the wrong money or none, the wrong paper,
maps of another town, the phrase book
for yesterday's language, just a ticket
to the next station, and my instructions.

In the lobby of the Banco Bilbao
a dark woman will slip me a key, a package,
the name of a hotel, a numbered account,
the first letters of an unknown alphabet.

Shadows

Zaro Weil

Moon
Last evening you
Rolled so loud and silver
Past my window
That the shadows
Woke and wove their dark
Molasses stripes
Over my bed

And
In the criss-cross of
That night-time
I knew what to do
Breathe soft
Breathe soft
And fold into a quiet silhouette
Until morning

Mending Wall

Robert Frost

Something there is that doesn't love a wall,
That sends the frozen-ground-swell under it,
And spills the upper boulders in the sun;
And makes gaps even two can pass abreast.
The work of hunters is another thing:
I have come after them and made repair
Where they have left not one stone on a stone,
But they would have the rabbit out of hiding,
To please the yelping dogs. The gaps I mean,
No one has seen them made or heard them made,
But at spring mending-time we find them there.
I let my neighbour know beyond the hill;
And on a day we meet to walk the line
And set the wall between us once again.
We keep the wall between us as we go.
To each the boulders that have fallen to each.
And some are loaves and some so nearly balls
We have to use a spell to make them balance:
'Stay where you are until our backs are turned!'
We wear our fingers rough with handling them.
Oh, just another kind of outdoor game,
One on a side. It comes to little more:
There where it is we do not need the wall:
He is all pine and I am apple orchard.
My apple trees will never get across
And eat the cones under his pines, I tell him.
He only says, 'Good fences make good neighbours.'
Spring is the mischief in me, and I wonder
If I could put a notion in his head:
'*Why* do they make good neighbours? Isn't it
Where there are cows? But here there are no cows.

Before I built a wall I'd ask to know
What I was walling in or walling out,
And to whom I was like to give offence.
Something there is that doesn't love a wall
That wants it down.' I could say 'Elves' to him,
But it's not elves exactly, and I'd rather
He said it for himself. I see him there
Bringing a stone grasped firmly by the top
In each hand, like an old-stone savage armed.
He moves in darkness as it seems to me,
Not of woods only and the shade of trees.
He will not go behind his father's saying,
And he likes having thought of it so well
He says again, 'Good fences make good neighbours.'

Wall

Norman Nicholson

The wall walks the fell—
Grey millipede on slow
Stone hooves;
Its slack back followed
At gulleys and grooves,
Or shouldering over
Old boulders
Too big to be rolled away.
Fallen fragments
Of the high crags
Crawl in the walk of the wall.

A dry-stone wall
Is a wall and a wall,
Leaning together
(Cumberland-and-Westmorland
Champion wrestlers),
Creening and weathering,
Flank by flank,
With filling of rubble
Between the two—
A double-rank
Stone dyke:
Flags and through—
stones jutting out sideways,
Like the step of a stile.

A wall walks slowly.
At each give of the ground,
Each creek of the rock's ribs
It puts its foot gingerly,
Arches its hog-holes,
Lets cobble and knee-joint
Settle and grip.
As the slipping fellside
Erodes and drifts,
The wall shifts with it,
Is always on the move.

They built a wall slowly,
A day a week;
Built it to stand,
But not stand still.
They built a wall to walk.

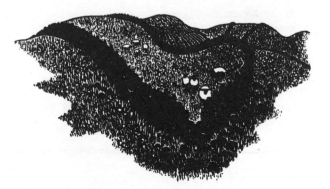

The Old Ships

James Elroy Flecker

I have seen old ships sail like swans asleep
Beyond the village which men still call Tyre,
With leaden age o'er-cargoed, dipping deep
For Famagusta and the hidden sun
That rings black Cyprus with a lake of fire;
And all those ships were certainly so old
Who knows how oft with squat and noisy gun,
Questing brown slaves or Syrian oranges,
The pirate Genoese
Hell-raked them till they rolled
Blood, water, fruit, and corpses up the hold.
But now through friendly seas they softly run,
Painted the mid-sea blue or shore-sea green,
Still patterned with the vine and grapes in gold.

But I have seen,
Pointing her shapely shadows from the dawn
And image-tumbled on a rose-swept bay,
A drowsy ship of some yet older day;
And, wonder's breath indrawn,
Thought I—who knows—who knows—but in that same
(Fished up beyond Ææa, patched up new
—Stern painted brighter blue—)
That talkative bald-headed seaman came
(Twelve patient comrades sweating at the oar)
From Troy's doom-crimson shore,
And with great lies about this wooden horse
Set the crew laughing, and forgot his course.

It was so old a ship—who knows, who knows?
—And yet so beautiful, I watched in vain
To see the mast burst open with a rose,
And the whole deck put on its leaves again.

Posted

John Masefield

Dream after dream I see the wrecks that lie
Unknown of man, unmarked upon the charts,
Known of the flat-fish with the withered eye,
And seen by women in their aching hearts.

World-wide the scattering is of those fair ships
That trod the billow tops till out of sight:
The cuttle mumbles them with horny lips,
The shells of the sea-insects crust them white.

In silence and in dimness and in greenness
Among the indistinct and leathery leaves
Of fruitless life they lie among the cleanness.
Fish glide and flit, slow under-movement heaves:

But no sound penetrates, not even the lunge
Of live ships passing, nor the gannet's plunge.

The Sea

James Reeves

The sea is a hungry dog,
Giant and grey.
He rolls on the beach all day.
With his clashing teeth and shaggy jaws
Hour upon hour he gnaws
The rumbling, tumbling stones,
And 'Bones, bones, bones, bones!'
The giant sea-dog moans,
Licking his greasy paws.

And when the night wind roars
And the moon rocks in the stormy cloud,
He bounds to his feet and snuffs and sniffs,
Shaking his wet sides over the cliffs,
And howls and hollos long and loud.

But on quiet days in May or June,
When even the grasses on the dune
Play no more their reedy tune,
With his head between his paws
He lies on the sandy shores,
So quiet, so quiet, he scarcely snores.

Look, No Hands

James Berry

Without muscles, without an arm or hand grip,
look how I wind bend back trees' big limbs.

Without wheels, without a down-hill,
look how I the sea roll and roll along.

Without a hurt, without a bruise,
look how I waterfall tumble down rocks.

Without bricks, without hammer or nails,
look how I tree build a house for birds.

Without apprenticeship, without DIY store,
look how I eagle build my family's nest.

Without getting even one single penny,
look how we apple trees give up our red apples.

Without a hose, without a sprinkler,
look how I sky water gardens with my rain.

WAR

Drummer Hodge

Thomas Hardy

I
They throw in Drummer Hodge, to rest
    Uncoffined—just as found:
His landmark is a kopje-crest
    That breaks the veldt around;
And foreign constellations west
    Each night above his mound.

II
Young Hodge the Drummer never knew—
    Fresh from his Wessex home—
The meaning of the broad Karoo,
    The Bush, the dusty loam,
And why uprose to nightly view
    Strange stars amid the gloom.

III
Yet portion of that unknown plain
    Will Hodge for ever be;
His homely Northern breast and brain
    Grow to some Southern tree,
And strange-eyed constellations reign
    His stars eternally.

Abbey Tomb

Patricia Beer

I told them not to ring the bells
The night the Vikings came
Out of the sea and passed us by.
The fog was thick as cream
And in the abbey we stood still
As if our breath might blare
Or pulses rattle if we once
Stopped staring at the door.

Through the walls and through the fog
We heard them passing by.
The deafer monks thanked God too soon
And later only I
Could catch the sound of prowling men
Still present in the hills
So everybody else agreed
To ring the abbey bells.

And even while the final clang
Still snored upon the air,
And while the ringers joked their way
Down round the spiral stair,
Before the spit of fervent prayer
Had dried into the stone
The raiders came back through the fog
And killed us one by one.

Father Abbot at the altar
Lay back with his knees
Doubled under him, caught napping
In the act of praise.
Brother John lay unresponsive
In the warming room.
The spiders came out for the heat
And then the rats for him.

Under the level of the sheep
Who graze here all the time
We lie now, under tourists' feet
Who in good weather come.
I told them not to ring the bells
But centuries of rain
And blustering have made their tombs
Look just as right as mine.

The Soldier
Rupert Brooke

If I should die, think only this of me:
   That there's some corner of a foreign field
That is for ever England. There shall be
   In that rich earth a richer dust concealed;
A dust whom England bore, shaped, made aware,
   Gave, once, her flowers to love, her ways to roam,
A body of England's, breathing English air,
   Washed by the rivers, blest by suns of home.

And think, this heart, all evil shed away,
   A pulse in the eternal mind, no less
      Gives somewhere back the thoughts by England given;
Her sights and sounds; dreams happy as her day;
   And laughter, learnt of friends; and gentleness,
      In hearts at peace, under an English heaven.

Newscast
Ian Hamilton

The Vietnam war drags on
In one corner of our living room.
The conversation turns
To take it in.
Our smoking heads
Drift back to us
From the grey fires of South East Asia.

My Boy Jack

Rudyard Kipling

'Have you news of my boy Jack?'
   Not this tide.
'When d'you think that he'll come back?'
   Not with this wind blowing, and this tide.

'Has anyone else had word of him?'
   Not this tide.
For what is sunk will hardly swim,
   Not with this wind blowing and this tide.

'Oh, dear, what comfort can I find?'
   None this tide,
   Nor any tide,
Except he did not shame his kind—
   Not even with that wind blowing, and that tide.

Then hold your head up all the more,
   This tide,
   And every tide;
Because he was the son you bore,
   And gave to that wind blowing and that tide!

As the Team's Head-Brass

Edward Thomas

As the team's head-brass flashed out on the turn
The lovers disappeared into the wood.
I sat among the boughs of the fallen elm
That strewed the angle of the fallow, and
Watched the plough narrowing a yellow square
Of charlock. Every time the horses turned
Instead of treading me down, the ploughman leaned
Upon the handles to say or ask a word,
About the weather, next about the war.
Scraping the share he faced towards the wood,
And screwed along the furrow till the brass flashed
Once more.
                    The blizzard felled the elm whose crest
I sat in, by a woodpecker's round hole,
The ploughman said. 'When will they take it away?'
'When the war's over.' So the talk began—
One minute and an interval of ten,
A minute more and the same interval.
'Have you been out?' 'No.' 'And don't want to,
      perhaps?'
'If I could only come back again, I should.
I could spare an arm. I shouldn't want to lose
A leg. If I should lose my head, why, so,
I should want nothing more. . . . Have many gone
From here?' 'Yes.' 'Many lost?' 'Yes, a good few.
Only two teams work on the farm this year.
One of my mates is dead. The second day
In France they killed him. It was back in March,
The very night of the blizzard, too. Now if
He had stayed here we should have moved the tree.'

'And I should not have sat here. Everything
Would have been different. For it would have been
Another world.' 'Ay, and a better, though
If we could see all all might seem good.' Then
The lovers came out of the wood again:
The horses started and for the last time
I watched the clods crumble and topple over
After the ploughshare and the stumbling team.

Anthem for Doomed Youth
Wilfred Owen

What passing-bells for these who die as cattle?
  Only the monstrous anger of the guns.
  Only the stuttering rifles' rapid rattle
Can patter out their hasty orisons.
No mockeries for them from prayers or bells,
  Nor any voice of mourning save the choirs,—
The shrill, demented choirs of wailing shells;
  And bugles calling for them from sad shires.

What candles may be held to speed them all?
  Not in the hands of boys, but in their eyes
Shall shine the holy glimmers of goodbyes.
  The pallor of girls' brows shall be their pall;
Their flowers the tenderness of silent minds,
And each slow dusk a drawing-down of blinds.

Naming of Parts

Henry Reed

Today we have naming of parts. Yesterday,
We had daily cleaning. And tomorrow morning,
We shall have what to do after firing. But today,
Today we have naming of parts. Japonica
Glistens like coral in all of the neighbouring gardens,
   And today we have naming of parts.

This is the lower sling swivel. And this
Is the upper sling swivel, whose use you will see,
When you are given your slings. And this is the piling swivel,
Which in your case you have not got. The branches
Hold in the gardens their silent, eloquent gestures,
   Which in our case we have not got.

This is the safety-catch, which is always released
With an easy flick of the thumb. And please do not let me
See anyone using his finger. You can do it quite easy
If you have any strength in your thumb. The blossoms
Are fragile and motionless, never letting anyone see
   Any of them using their finger.

And this you can see is the bolt. The purpose of this
Is to open the breech, as you see. We can slide it
Rapidly backwards and forwards: we call this
Easing the spring. And rapidly backwards and forwards
The early bees are assaulting and fumbling the flowers:
   They call it easing the Spring.

They call it easing the Spring: it is perfectly easy
If you have any strength in your thumb: like the bolt,
And the breech, and the cocking-piece, and the point of balance,
Which in our case we have not got; and the almond-blossom
Silent in all of the gardens and the bees going backwards and
    forwards,
   For today we have naming of parts.

Vergissmeinnicht

Keith Douglas

Three weeks gone and the combatants gone,
returning over the nightmare ground
we found the place again, and found
the soldier sprawling in the sun.

The frowning barrel of his gun
overshadowing. As we came on
that day, he hit my tank with one
like the entry of a demon.

Look. Here in the gunpit spoil
the dishonoured picture of his girl
who has put: *Steffi. Vergissmeinnicht*
in a copybook gothic script.

We see him almost with content,
abased, and seeming to have paid
and mocked at by his own equipment
that's hard and good when he's decayed.

But she would weep to see today
how on his skin the swart flies move;
the dust upon the paper eye
and the burst stomach like a cave.

For here the lover and killer are mingled
who had one body and one heart.
And death who had the soldier singled
has done the lover mortal hurt.

Your Attention Please

Peter Porter

The Polar DEW has just warned that
A nuclear rocket strike of
At least one thousand megatons
Has been launched by the enemy
Directly at our major cities.
This announcement will take
Two and a quarter minutes to make,
You therefore have a further
Eight and a quarter minutes
To comply with the shelter
Requirements published in the Civil
Defence Code—section Atomic Attack.
A specially shortened Mass
Will be broadcast at the end
Of this announcement—
Protestant and Jewish services
Will begin simultaneously—
Select your wavelength immediately
According to instructions
In the Defence Code. Do not
Take well-loved pets (including birds)
Into your shelter—they will consume
Fresh air. Leave the old and bed-
ridden, you can do nothing for them.
Remember to press the sealing
Switch when everyone is in
The shelter. Set the radiation
Aerial, turn on the geiger barometer.
Turn off your television now.

Turn off your radio immediately
The Services end. At the same time
Secure explosion plugs in the ears
Of each member of your family. Take
Down your plasma flasks. Give your children
The pills marked one and two
In the C.D. green container, then put
Them to bed. Do not break
The inside airlock seals until
The radiation All Clear shows
(Watch for the cuckoo in your
perspex panel), or your District
Touring Doctor rings your bell.
If before this, your air becomes
Exhausted or if any of your family
Is critically injured, administer
The capsules marked 'Valley Forge'
(Red pocket in No. 1 Survival Kit)
For painless death. (Catholics
Will have been instructed by their priests
What to do in this eventuality.)
This announcement is ending. Our President
Has already given orders for
Massive retaliation—it will be
Decisive. Some of us may die.
Remember, statistically
It is not likely to be you.
All flags are flying fully dressed
On Government buildings—the sun is shining.
Death is the least we have to fear.
We are all in the hands of God,
Whatever happens happens by His Will.
Now go quickly to your shelters.

No More Hiroshimas

James Kirkup

At the station exit, my bundle in hand,
Early the winter afternoon's wet snow
Falls thinly round me, out of a crudded sun.
I had forgotten to remember where I was.
Looking about, I see it might be anywhere—
A station, a town like any other in Japan,
Ramshackle, muddy, noisy, drab; a cheerfully
Shallow permanence: peeling concrete, litter, 'Atomic
Lotion, for hair fall-out,' a flimsy department-store;
Racks and towers of neon, flashy over tiled and tilted waves
Of little roofs, shacks cascading lemons and persimmons,
Oranges and dark-red apples, shanties awash with rainbows
Of squid and octopus, shellfish, slabs of tuna, oysters, ice,
Ablaze with fans of soiled nude-picture books
Thumbed abstractedly by schoolboys, with second-hand looks.

The river remains unchanged, sad, refusing rehabilitation.
In this long, wide, empty official boulevard
The new trees are still small, the office blocks
Basely functional, the bridge a slick abstraction.
But the river remains unchanged; sad, refusing rehabilitation.

In the city centre, far from the station's lively squalor,
A kind of life goes on, in cinemas and hi-fi coffee bars,
In the shuffling racket of pin-table palaces and parlours,
The souvenir-shops piled with junk, kimonoed kewpie-dolls,
Models of the bombed Industry Promotion Hall, memorial ruin
Tricked out with glitter-frost and artificial pearls.

Set in an awful emptiness, the modern tourist hotel is trimmed
With jaded Christmas frippery, flatulent balloons; in the hall,
A giant dingy iced cake in the shape of a Cinderella coach.
The contemporary stairs are treacherous, the corridors
Deserted, my room an overheated morgue, the bar in darkness.

Punctually, the electric chimes ring out across the tidy waste
Their doleful public hymn—the tune unrecognizable, evangelist.

Here atomic peace is geared to meet the tourist trade.
Let it remain like this, for all the world to see,
Without nobility or loveliness, and dogged with shame
That is beyond all hope of indignation. Anger, too, is dead.
And why should memorials of what was far
From pleasant have the grace that helps us to forget?

In the dying afternoon, I wander dying round the Park of Peace.
It is right, this squat, dead place, with its left-over air
Of an abandoned International Trade and Tourist Fair.
The stunted trees are wrapped in straw against the cold.
The gardeners are old, old women in blue bloomers, white aprons,
Survivors weeding the dead brown lawns around the Children's
Monument.

A hideous pile, the Atomic Bomb Explosion Centre, freezing cold,
'Includes the Peace Tower, a museum containing
Atomic-melted slates and bricks, photos showing
What the Atomic Desert looked like, and other
Relics of the catastrophe.'

The other relics:
The ones that made me weep;
The bits of burnt clothing,
The stopped watches, the torn shirts.
The twisted buttons,
The stained and tattered vests and drawers,
The ripped kimonos and charred boots,
The white blouse polka-dotted with atomic rain, indelible,
The cotton summer pants the blasted boys crawled home in, to bleed
And slowly die.

Remember only these.
They are the memorials we need.

Fifteen Million Plastic Bags

Adrian Mitchell

I was walking in a government warehouse
Where the daylight never goes.
I saw fifteen million plastic bags
Hanging in a thousand rows.

Five million bags were six feet long
Five million were five foot five
Five million were stamped with Mickey Mouse
And they came in a smaller size.

Were they for guns or uniforms
Or a dirty kind of party game?
Then I saw each bag had a number
And every bag bore a name.

And five million bags were six feet long
Five million were five foot five
Five million were stamped with Mickey Mouse
And they came in a smaller size.

So I've taken my bag from the hanger
And I've pulled it over my head
And I'll wait for the priest to zip it
So the radiation won't spread.

Now five million bags are six feet long
Five million are five foot five
Five million are stamped with Mickey Mouse
And they come in a smaller size.

In the Desert Knowing Nothing

Helen Dunmore

Here I am in the desert knowing nothing,
here I am knowing nothing
in the desert of knowing nothing,
here I am in this wide
desert long after midnight.

here I am knowing nothing
hearing the noise of the rain
and the melt of fat in the pan

here is our man on the phone knowing something
and here's our man fresh from the briefing
in combat jeans and a clip microphone
testing for sound,
catching the desert rain, knowing something,

here's the general who's good with his men
storming the camera, knowing something
in the pit of his Americanness
here's the general taut in his battledress
and knowing something

Here's the boy washing his kit in a tarpaulin
on a front-line he knows from his GCSE
coursework on Wilfred Owen
and knowing something

here is the plane banking,
the *go go go* of adrenalin
the child melting
and here's the grass that grows overnight
from the desert rain, feeling for him
and knowing everything

and here I am knowing nothing
in the desert of knowing nothing
dry from not speaking.

Carriers in the Gulf

Alan Ross

Huge ironing-board with stuck-on insects
   Ready on order to peel off
     They suggest
  Waterborne coffins searching graveyards.
Oceans part like surplices, silver reflects

Off strut, fuselage, wing, aerial.
   Overlooked, or from afar
     Through binoculars,
  Planes seem balsa and glue heat
Might melt as they trundle towards hangars,
   Crews crouched in attitudes of burial.

Raked bows that slit rainbow-oiled wakes
   From tankers ahead of them, flare
     Of their fo'c'sles
  Delivers into shade as though awnings
   Busy accomplices—oilers,
Pinnaces, grateful of respite from glare.

About their lawful or invidious purposes
   At one with flying fish and dolphin
     They scatter aircraft
  At sunset, the sky white with confetti,
Gulls settling on their ballroom of raft.

A poem about Poems About Vietnam

Jon Stallworthy

The spotlights had you covered [*thunder
in the wings*]. In the combat zones
and in the Circle, darkness. Under
the muzzles of the microphones
you opened fire, and a phalanx
of loudspeakers shook on the wall;
but all your cartridges were blanks
when you were at the Albert Hall.

Lord George Byron cared for Greece,
Auden and Cornford cared for Spain,
confronted bullets and disease
to make their poems' meaning plain;
but you—by what right did you wear
suffering like a service medal,
numbing the nerve that they laid bare,
when you were at the Albert Hall?

The poets of another time—
Owen with a rifle-butt
between his paper and the slime,
Donne quitting Her pillow to cut
a quill—knew that in love and war
dispatches from the front are all.
We believe them, they were there,
when you were at the Albert Hall.

Poet, they whisper in their sleep
louder from underground than all
the mikes that hung upon your lips
when you were at the Albert Hall.

Tiananmen

James Fenton

Tiananmen
Is broad and clean
And you can't tell
Where the dead have been
And you can't tell
What happened then
And you can't speak
Of Tiananmen.

You must not speak.
You must not think.
You must not dip
Your brush in ink.
You must not say
When happened then,
What happened there
In Tiananmen.

The cruel men
Are old and deaf
Ready to kill
But short of breath
And they will die
Like other men
And they'll lie in state
In Tiananmen.

They lie in state.
They lie in style.
Another lie's
Thrown on the pile,
Thrown on the pile
By the cruel men
To cleanse the blood
From Tiananmen.

Truth is a secret.
Keep it dark.
Keep it dark
In your heart of hearts.
Keep in dark
Till you know when
Truth may return
To Tiananmen.

Tiananmen
Is broad and clean
And you can't tell
Where the dead have been
And you can't tell
When they'll come again.
They'll come again
To Tiananmen.

The Sunlight on the Garden

Louis MacNeice

The sunlight on the garden
Hardens and grows cold,
We cannot cage the minute
Within its nets of gold,
When all is told
We cannot beg for pardon.

Our freedom as free lances
Advances towards its end;
The earth compels, upon it
Sonnets and birds descend;
And soon, my friend,
We shall have no time for dances.

The sky was good for flying
Defying the church bells
And every evil iron
Siren and what it tells:
The earth compels,
We are dying, Egypt, dying

And not expecting pardon,
Hardened in heart anew,
But glad to have sat under
Thunder and rain with you,
And grateful too
For sunlight on the garden.

LOVE

I so liked Spring

Charlotte Mew

I so liked Spring last year
    Because you were here;—
        The thrushes too—
Because it was these you so liked to hear—
        I so liked you.

This year's a different thing,—
        I'll not think of you.
But I'll like Spring because it is simply Spring
        As the thrushes do.

The River-Merchant's Wife: A Letter

Ezra Pound

While my hair was still cut straight across my forehead
I played about the front gate, pulling flowers.
You came by on bamboo stilts, playing horse,
You walked about my seat, playing with blue plums.
And we went on living in the village of Chokan:
Two small people, without dislike or suspicion.

At fourteen I married My Lord you.
I never laughed, being bashful.
Lowering my head, I looked at the wall.
Called to, a thousand times, I never looked back.

At fifteen I stopped scowling,
I desired my dust to be mingled with yours
Forever and forever and forever.
Why should I climb the look out?

At sixteen you departed,
You went into far Ku-to-yen, by the river of swirling eddies,
And you have been gone five months.
The monkeys make sorrowful noise overhead.

You dragged your feet when you went out.
By the gate now, the moss is grown, the different mosses,
Too deep to clear them away!
The leaves fall early this autumn, in wind.
The paired butterflies are already yellow with August
Over the grass in the West garden;
They hurt me. I grow older.
If you are coming down through the narrows of the river Kiang,
Please let me know beforehand,
And I will come out to meet you
        As far as Cho-fu-Sa.

                             By Rihaku

Like a Flame

Grace Nichols

Raising up
from my weeding
of ripening cane

my eyes
make four
with this man

there ain't
no reason
to laugh

but
I laughing
in confusion

his hands
soft his words
quick his lips
curling as in
prayer

I nod

I like this man

Tonight
I go to meet him
like a flame.

First Love
Brian Patten

Sarah's my girlfriend,
Without her I feel
Like a ball with no bounce,
A shoe with no heel,
An up with no down,
A snow with no flake,
A fish trying to swim
In a waterless lake.
Sarah's my girlfriend,
Without her I fear
I feel that I'm nowhere,
Especially not here.

Lipservice
Max Fatchen

Our lips,
Are meant for hisses
And kisses,
Wisecracks
And quips
But mine are mostly
For fish and chips.

Love Poem

Mick Gowar

If I can get from here   to the pillar box
If I can get from here   to the lamp-post
If I can get from here to the front gate
  before a car comes round the corner . . .
Carolyn Murray will come to tea
Carolyn Murray will   love me too
Carolyn Murray will   marry me
But only if I get from here to there
  before a car comes round the corner . . .

Any prince to any princess

Adrian Henri

August is coming
and the goose, I'm afraid,
is getting fat.
There have been
no golden eggs for some months now.
Straw has fallen well below market price
despite my frantic spinning
and the sedge is,
as you rightly point out,
withered.

I can't imagine how the pea
got under your mattress. I apologize
humbly. The chambermaid has, of course,
been sacked. As has the frog footman.
I understand that, during my recent fact-finding tour of the
    Golden River,
despite your nightly unavailing efforts,
he remained obstinately
froggish.

I hope that the Three Wishes granted by the General
    Assembly
will go some way towards redressing
this unfortunate recent sequence of events.
The fall in output from the shoe-factory, for example:
no one could have foreseen the work-to-rule
by the National Union of Elves. Not to mention the fact
that the court has been fast asleep
for the last six and a half years.

The matter of the poisoned apple has been taken up
by the Board of Trade: I think I can assure you
the incident will not be
repeated.

I can quite understand, in the circumstances,
your reluctance to let down
your golden tresses. However
I feel I must point out
that the weather isn't getting any better
and I already have a nasty chill
from waiting at the base
of the White Tower. You must see the absurdity of the
    situation.
Some of the courtiers are beginning to talk,
not to mention the humble villagers.
It's been three weeks now, and not even
a word.

Princess,
a cold, black wind
howls through our empty palace.
Dead leaves litter the bedchamber;
the mirror on the wall hasn't said a thing
since you left. I can only ask,
bearing all this in mind,
that you think again,

let down your hair,

reconsider.

A Subaltern's Love-song

John Betjeman

Miss J. Hunter Dunn, Miss J. Hunter Dunn,
Furnish'd and burnish'd by Aldershot sun,
What strenuous singles we played after tea,
We in the tournament—you against me!

Love-thirty, love-forty, oh! weakness of joy,
The speed of a swallow, the grace of a boy,
With carefullest carelessness, gaily you won,
I am weak from your loveliness, Joan Hunter Dunn.

Miss Joan Hunter Dunn, Miss Joan Hunter Dunn,
How mad I am, sad I am, glad that you won.
The warm-handled racket is back in its press,
But my shock-headed victor, she loves me no less.

Her father's euonymus shines as we walk,
And swing past the summer-house, buried in talk,
And cool the verandah that welcomes us in
To the six-o'clock news and a lime-juice and gin.

The scent of the conifers, sound of the bath,
The view from my bedroom of moss-dappled path,
As I struggle with double-end evening tie,
For we dance at the Golf Club, my victor and I.

On the floor of her bedroom lie blazer and shorts
And the cream-coloured walls are be-trophied with sports,
And westering, questioning settles the sun
On your low-leaded window, Miss Joan Hunter Dunn.

The Hillman is waiting, the light's in the hall,
The pictures of Egypt are bright on the wall,
My sweet, I am standing beside the oak stair
And there on the landing's the light on your hair.

By roads 'not adopted', by woodlanded ways,
She drove to the club in the late summer haze,
Into nine-o'clock Camberley, heavy with bells
And mushroomy, pine-woody, evergreen smells.

Miss Joan Hunter Dunn, Miss Joan Hunter Dunn,
I can hear from the car park the dance has begun.
Oh! full Surrey twilight! importunate band!
Oh! strongly adorable tennis-girl's hand!

Around us are Rovers and Austins afar,
Above us, the intimate roof of the car,
And here on my right is the girl of my choice,
With the tilt of her nose and the chime of her voice,

And the scent of her wrap, and the words never said,
And the ominous, ominous dancing ahead.
We sat in the car park till twenty to one
And now I'm engaged to Miss Joan Hunter Dunn.

Tarantella

Hilaire Belloc

Do you remember an Inn,
Miranda?
Do you remember an Inn?
And the tedding and the spreading
Of the straw for a bedding,
And the fleas that tease in the High Pyrenees,
And the wine that tasted of the tar,
And the cheers and the jeers of the young muleteers
(Under the vine of the dark verandah)?
Do you remember an Inn, Miranda,
Do you remember an Inn?
And the cheers and the jeers of the young muleteers
Who hadn't got a penny,
And who weren't paying any,
And the hammer at the doors and the Din?

And the Hip! Hop! Hap!
Of the clap
Of the hands to the twirl and the swirl
Of the girl gone chancing,
Glancing,
Dancing,
Backing and advancing,
Snapping of the clapper to the spin
Out and in—
And the Ting, Tong, Tang of the Guitar!
Do you remember an Inn,
Miranda?
Do you remember an Inn?

Never more,
Miranda,
Never more.
Only the high peaks hoar:
And Aragon a torrent at the door.
No sound
In the walls of the Halls where falls
The tread
Of the feet of the dead to the ground,
No sound:
But the boom
Of the far Waterfall like Doom.

Water

Robert Lowell

It was a Maine lobster-town—
Each morning boatloads of hands
pushed off for granite
quarries on the islands,

and left dozens of bleak
white frame houses stuck
like oyster shells
on a hill of rock,

and below us, the sea lapped
the raw little match-stick
mazes of a weir
where the fish for bait were trapped.

Remember? We sat on a slab of rock.
From this distance in time,
it seems the color
of iris, rotting and turning purpler,

but it was only
the usual gray rock
turning the usual green
when drenched by the sea.

The sea drenched the rock
at our feet all day,
and kept tearing away
flake after flake.

One night you dreamed
you were a mermaid clinging to a wharf-pile,
and trying to pull
off the barnacles with your hands.
We wished our two souls
might return like gulls
to the rock. In the end,
the water was too cold for us.

No Sense of Direction

Vernon Scannell

I have always admired
Those who are sure
Which turning to take,
Who need no guide
Even in war
When thunders shake
The torn terrain,
When battalions of shrill
Stars all desert
And the derelict moon
Goes over the hill:
Eyes chained by the night
They find their way back
As if it were daylight.
Then, on peaceful walks
Over strange wooded ground,

They will find the right track,
Know which of the forks
Will lead to the inn
I would never have found;
For I lack their gift,
Possess almost no
Sense of direction.
And yet I owe
A debt to this lack,
A debt so vast
No reparation
Can ever be made,
For it led me away
From the road I sought
Which would carry me to—
I mistakenly thought—
My true destination:
It made me stray
To this lucky path
That ran like a fuse
And brought me to you

And love's bright, soundless
Detonation.

Valentine

Carol Ann Duffy

Not a red rose or a satin heart.

I give you an onion.
It is a moon wrapped in brown paper.
It promises light
like the careful undressing of love.

Here.
It will blind you with tears
like a lover.
It will make your reflection
a wobbling photo of grief.

I am trying to be truthful.

Not a cute card or a kissogram.

I give you an onion.
Its fierce kiss will stay on your lips,
possessive and faithful
as we are,
for as long as we are.

Take it.
Its platinum loops shrink to a wedding-ring,
if you like.
Lethal.
Its scent will cling to your fingers,
cling to your knife.

The Highwayman
Alfred Noyes

Part I

The wind was a torrent of darkness among the gusty trees,
The moon was a ghostly galleon tossed upon cloudy seas.
The road was a ribbon of moonlight over the purple moor,
And the highwayman came riding—
    Riding—riding—
The highwayman came riding, up to the old inn-door.

He'd a French cocked-hat on his forehead, a bunch of lace at his
   chin,
A coat of the claret velvet, and breeches of brown doe-skin.
They fitted with never a wrinkle. His boots were up to the thigh.
And he rode with a jewelled twinkle,
    His pistol butts a-twinkle,
His rapier hilt a-twinkle, under the jewelled sky.

Over the cobbles he clattered and clashed in the dark inn-yard.
He tapped with his whip on the shutters, but all was locked and
   barred.
He whistled a tune to the window, and who should be waiting there
But the landlord's black-eyed daughter,
    Bess, the landlord's daughter,
Plaiting a dark red love-knot into her long black hair.

And dark in the dark old inn-yard a stable-wicket creaked
Where Tim the ostler listened. His face was white and peaked.
His eyes were hollows of madness, his hair like mouldy hay,
But he loved the landlord's daughter,
    The landlord's red-lipped daughter.
Dumb as a dog he listened, and he heard the robber say—

'One kiss, my bonny sweetheart, I'm after a prize tonight,
But I shall be back with the yellow gold before the morning
   light;
Yet, if they press me sharply, and harry me through the day,
Then look for me by moonlight,
     Watch for me by moonlight,
I'll come to thee by moonlight, though hell should bar the way.'

He rose upright in the stirrups. He scarce could reach her hand,
But she loosened her hair i' the casement. His face burnt like a brand
As the black cascade of perfume came tumbling over his breast;
And he kissed its waves in the moonlight,
     (Oh, sweet black waves in the moonlight!)
Then he tugged at his rein in the moonlight, and galloped away
   to the west.

Part II

He did not come in the dawning. He did not come at noon;
And out o' the tawny sunset, before the rise o' the moon,
When the road was a gipsy's ribbon, looping the purple moor,
A red-coat troop came marching—
     Marching—marching—
King George's men came marching, up to the old inn-door.

They said no word to the landlord. They drank his ale instead.
But they gagged his daughter, and bound her, to the foot of her
   narrow bed.
Two of them knelt at her casement, with muskets at their side!
There was death at every window;
     And hell at one dark window;
For Bess could see, through her casement, the road that *he* would
   ride.

They had tied her up to attention, with many a sniggering jest.
They had bound a musket beside her, with the muzzle beneath her
    breast!
'Now, keep good watch!' and they kissed her.
        She heard the dead man say—
Look for me by moonlight;
    Watch for me by moonlight;
I'll come to thee by moonlight, though hell should bar the way!

She twisted her hands behind her; but all the knots held good!
She writhed her hands till her fingers were wet with sweat or blood!
They stretched and strained in the darkness, and the hours crawled
    by like years,
Till, now, on the stroke of midnight,
        Cold, on the stroke of midnight,
The tip of one finger touched it! The trigger at least was hers!

The tip of one finger touched it. She strove no more for the rest.
Up, she stood up to attention, with the muzzle beneath her breast.
She would not risk their hearing, she would not strive again;
For the road lay bare in the moonlight;
        Blank and bare in the moonlight;
And the blood of her veins, in the moonlight, throbbed to her love's
    refrain.

Tlot-tlot; tlot-tlot! Had they heard it? The horse-hoofs ringing clear;
Tlot-tlot, tlot-tlot, in the distance! Were they deaf that they did not
    hear?
Down the ribbon of moonlight, over the brow of the hill,
The highwayman came riding,
        Riding, riding!
The red-coats looked to their priming! She stood up, straight and still.

Tlot-tlot, in the frosty silence! *Tlot-tlot*, in the echoing night!
Nearer he came and nearer. Her face was like a light.
Her eyes grew wide for a moment; she drew one last deep breath,

Then her finger moved in the moonlight,
    Her musket shattered the moonlight,
Shattered her breast in the moonlight and warned him—with her death.

He turned. He spurred to the west; he did not know who stood
Bowed, with her head o'er the musket, drenched with her own red
    blood!
Not till the dawn he heard it, and his face grew grey to hear
How Bess, the landlord's daughter,
    The landlord's black-eyed daughter,
Had watched for her love in the moonlight, and died in the darkness
    there.

Back, he spurred like a madman, shouting a curse to the sky,
With the white road smoking behind him and his rapier brandished
    high.
Blood-red were his spurs i' the golden noon; wine-red was his velvet
    coat;
When they shot him down on the highway,
    Down like a dog on the highway,
And he lay in his blood on the highway, with the bunch of lace at his
    throat.

And still of a winter's night, they say, when the wind is in the trees,
When the moon is a ghostly galleon tossed upon cloudy seas,
When the road is a ribbon of moonlight over the purple moor,
A highwayman comes riding—
    Riding—riding—
A highwayman comes riding, up to the old inn-door.

Over the cobbles he clatters and clangs in the dark inn-yard.
And he taps with his whip on the shutters, but all is locked and barred.
He whistles a tune to the window, and who should be waiting there
But the landlord's black-eyed daughter,
    Bess, the landlord's daughter,
Plaiting a dark red love-knot into her long black hair.

An Arundel Tomb

Philip Larkin

Side by side, their faces blurred,
The earl and countess lie in stone,
Their proper habits vaguely shown
As jointed armour, stiffened pleat,
And that faint hint of the absurd—
The little dogs under their feet.

Such plainness of the pre-baroque
Hardly involves the eye, until
It meets his left-hand gauntlet, still
Clasped empty in the other; and
One sees, with a sharp tender shock,
His hand withdrawn, holding her hand.

They would not think to lie so long.
Such faithfulness in effigy
Was just a detail friends would see:
A sculptor's sweet commissioned grace
Thrown off in helping to prolong
The Latin names around the base.

They would not guess how early in
Their supine stationary voyage
The air would change to soundless damage,
Turn the old tenantry away;
How soon succeeding eyes begin
To look, not read. Rigidly they

Persisted, linked, through lengths and breadths
Of time. Snow fell, undated. Light
Each summer thronged the glass. A bright
Litter of birdcalls strewed the same
Bone-riddled ground. And up the paths
The endless altered people came,
Washing at their identity.

Now, helpless in the hollow of
An unarmorial age, a trough
Of smoke in slow suspended skeins
Above their scrap of history,
Only an attitude remains:

Time has transfigured them into
Untruth. The stone fidelity
They hardly meant has come to be
Their final blazon, and to prove
Our almost-instinct almost true:
What will survive of us is love.

He Wishes for the Cloths of Heaven

W. B. Yeats

Had I the heavens' embroidered cloths,
Enwrought with golden and silver light,
The blue and the dim and the dark cloths
Of night and light and the half-light,
I would spread the cloths under your feet:
But I, being poor, have only my dreams;
I have spread my dreams under your feet;
Tread softly because you tread on my dreams.

Sometimes

Sheenagh Pugh

Sometimes things don't go, after all,
from bad to worse. Some years, muscadel
faces down frost; green thrives; the crops don't fail,
sometimes a man aims high, and all goes well.

A people sometimes will step back from war;
elect an honest man; decide they care
enough, that they can't leave some stranger poor.
Some men become what they were born for.

Sometimes our best efforts do not go
amiss; sometimes we do as we meant to.
The sun will sometimes melt a field of sorrow
that seemed hard frozen: may it happen for you.

Index of Titles and First Lines

First lines are in italics

A snail is climbing up the window-sill 55
A tourist came in from Orbitville 125
Abbey Tomb 142
About Friends 87
About His Person 96
Adventures of Isabel 60
Alice and the Frog 18
And she, being old, fed from a mashed plate 108
Animals' Arrival, The 33
Anthem for Doomed Youth 147
Any prince to any princess 166
April Rain Song 115
Arundel Tomb, An 180
As the cat/climbed over 47
As the Team's Head-Brass 146
As the team's head-brass flashed out on the turn 146
At the station exit, my bundle in hand 153
August is coming 166
Before it starts, she winds the window 66
Boyhood of Dracula, The 14
Broad sun-stoned beaches 117
Bury her deep, down deep 44
'But that was nothing to what things came out 24
By St Thomas Water 75
Call alligator long-mouth 38
Car Wash 66
Caring for Animals 54
Carriers in the Gulf 157
Cat's Funeral 44
Cat, if you go outdoors, you must walk in the snow 121
Caxtons are mechanical birds with many wings 111
Child's Calendar, A 79
Come visit my pancake collection 16
Considering the Snail 35
Day of These Days 116
Day the World Ended, The 126
Dialogue Between Ghost and Priest 26
Do you remember an Inn 170
Dog Body and Cat Mind 46
Don't Call Alligator Long-Mouth Till You Cross River 38
Donkey, The 51
Doomed Spaceman, The 110
Dream after dream I see the wrecks that lie 138
Drummer Hodge 141
Embankment, The 99
Encounter at St Martin's 130

Evans 105
Evans? Yes, many a time 105
Every Day in Every Way 98
Everyone Sang 32
Everyone suddenly burst out singing 32
Example, The 34
Father Says 62
Fern Hill 73
Fetching Cows 52
Fifteen Million Plastic Bags 155
First Love 164
First Men on Mercury, The 92
Five pounds fifty in change, exactly 96
Flower-Fed Buffaloes, The 53
Fog 120
Follower 84
For a Five-year-old 55
For the Record 113
Frog Prince, The 17
Frost called to water 'Halt!' 118
Game of Life, The 58
glancing away 113
Great Black-Backed Gulls 30
Had I the heavens' embroidered cloths 182
Hard Frost 118
Have you been in sight of heaven 58
'Have you news of my boy Jack?' 145
He was cold as slime 17
He Wishes for the Cloths of Heaven 182
Here I am in the desert knowing nothing 156
Here's an example from 34
Highwayman, The 176
Horses 50
Horses on the Camargue 48
Huge ironing-board with stuck-on insects 157
Hunger 103
I ask sometimes why these small animals 54
I come among the people like a shadow 103
I got up on the wrong side of the day 15
I have always admired 173
I have seen old ships sail like swans asleep 136
I hear a sudden cry of pain 43
I imagine this midnight moment's forest 45
I remember once being shown the black bull 80
I remember one winter-night meadow 110
I so liked Spring 161
I so liked Spring last year 161
I tell a wanderer's tale, the same 130
I told them not to ring the bells 142

I wanna be the leader   91
I was walking in a government warehouse   155
I Wish I Were . . .   77
I'll tell you, shall I, something I remember   56
Icing Hand, The   85
If I can get from here to the pillar box   165
If I got out of my grave   94
If I should die, think only this of me   144
in Just-spring   114
In moving-slow he has no Peer   36
In the cloakroom/Wet coats   64
In the Desert Knowing Nothing   156
In the grey wastes of dread   48
In the ice-trap of January   38
In the rectory garden on his evening walk   26
Into My Heart   72
Into my heart an air that kills   72
'Is there anybody there?' said the Traveller   22
Isabel met an enormous bear   60
It is eighteen years ago, almost to the day   90
It was a Maine lobster town   172
It Was Long Ago   56
Last night, while I lay thinking here   11
Leader, The   91
Legend   88
Lesson, The   83
Let the rain kiss you   115
library   9
Like a Flame   163
Lipservice   164
Listeners, The   22
London Snow   122
Look, No Hands   140
Lost Days   78
Love Poem   165
Loving words clutch crimson roses   10
Man on the Desert Island, The   100
Martian Sends a Postcard Home, A   111
Mary Celeste   28
Men of Terry Street   97
Mending Wall   132
Midnight Skaters, The   119
Midsummer, Tobago   117
Miss J. Hunter-Dunn, Miss J. Hunter-Dunn   168
Moon/Last evening you   131
Most people know   12
Mr McTaggart, good McTaggart   95
My Boy Jack   145
My father worked with a horse-plough   84
My father's friend came once to tea   82
Naming of Parts   148
Newscast   144
No More Hiroshimas   153
No need even   9

No Sense of Direction   173
No visitors in January   79
Nobody heard him, the dead man   101
Not a red rose or a satin heart   175
Not My Best Side   106
Not my best side, I'm afraid   106
Not My Day   15
Not Waving but Drowning   101
Now as I was young and easy under the apple boughs   73
O What is That Sound   104
O what is that sound which so thrills the ear   104
Old Ships, The   136
Old Woman   108
On a Night of Snow   121
Once, in finesse of fiddles found I ecstasy   99
Once upon a time/a princess called Alice   18
Only the wind sings   28
Our lips/Are meant for hisses   164
Pancake Collector, The   16
Piano   86
Pitying Heaven   95
Playgrounds   63
Playgrounds are such gobby places   63
Poem   47
poem about Poems about Vietnam, A   158
Posted   138
Preludes   128
Raising up/from my weeding   163
Recollection, A   82
Resurrected   94
Revelation   80
River-Merchant's Wife: A Letter, The   162
Said Cap'n Morgan to Cap'n Kidd   30
Sarah's my girlfriend   164
Sea, The   139
Sensitive, Seldom, and Sad   109
Shadows   131
She says 'How was you?' Kissing. 'Come on in   81
Shoes, The   70
Side by side, their faces blurred   180
Side Way Back, The   124
Sloth, The   36
Snare, The   43
So they came   33
So we let him join us   14
Softly, in the dusk, a woman is singing to me   86
Soldier, The   144
Something there is that doesn't love a wall   132
Something Told the Wild Geese   37
Sometimes   183
Sometimes things don't go, after all   183
Song of the Battery Hen   42
Southbound on the Freeway   125

Spell Against Sorrow   21
Spell for Midnight, A   20
Sticks and stones may break my bones   65
Subaltern's Love-song, A   168
Such a morning it is when love   116
Sunlight on the Garden, The   160
Tarantella   170
Televised   69
Televised news turns   69
That they lasted only till the next high tide 85
The black one, last as usual, swings her head 52
The blacksmith's boy went out with a rifle 88
The dog body and cat mind   46
The flower-fed buffaloes of the spring   53
The fog comes   120
The good thing about friends   87
The hop-poles stand in cones   119
The man on the desert island   100
The More It Snows   120
The Polar DEW *has just warned that*   151
The sea is a hungry dog   139
The snail pushes through a green   35
The spotlights had you covered   158
The sunlight on the garden   160
The Vietnam war drags on   144
The wall walks the fell   134
The washing machine was whirling away 126
The wind was a torrent of darkness among the gusty trees   176
The winter evening settles down   128
Then, when an hour was twenty hours, he lay 78
'There Will Come Soft Rains'   115
There will come soft rains and the smell of the ground   115
These are the shoes   70
They Call to One Another   31
They come in at night, leave in the early morning   97
They throw in Drummer Hodge, to rest   141
This is the way that I have to go   67
Those lumbering horses in the steady plough 50
Thought-Fox, The   45
Three weeks gone and the combatants gone 150
Tiananmen   159
Tickle Rhyme, The   34
Tich Miller   68
Tich Miller wore glasses   68
Today we have naming of parts. Yesterday 148
Trophy   38
Truth   65

Tunnel, The   67
Unrecorded Speech   81
Valentine   175
Vergissmeinnicht   150
Walking Away   90
Wall   134
Water   172
We are Going to See the Rabbit   40
We can't grumble about accommodation   42
We come in peace from the third planet   92
Welsh Incident   24
What passing-bells for these who die as cattle 147
What's What   12
Whatif   11
When fishes flew and forests walked   51
When I got up this morning   98
When I Was Christened   59
When men were all asleep the snow came flying   122
When Skies are Low and Days are Dark   123
When the gong sounds ten in the morning and I   77
Where's Everybody?   64
While my hair was still cut straight across my forehead   162
Who will take away   21
'Who's that tickling my back?' said the wall 34
Why Brownlee Left   102
Why Brownlee left, and where he went   102
Without muscles, without an arm or hand grip 140
Word Party, The   10
Yesterday is safe   20
You're late. Take a chance up the cul-de-sac 124
Your Attention Please   151
'*Your father's gone,*' *my bald headmaster said* 83

Index of Authors

Adams, Anna (b.1926)   81
Adcock, Fleur (b.1934)   55
Agard, John (b.1949)   38
Ahlberg, Allan (b.1938)   64
Angelou, Maya (b.1928)   69
Armitage, Simon (b.1963)   96
Auden, W. H. (1907–73)   104

Baldwin, Michael (b.1930)   95
Barker, George (1913–91)   31
Beer, Patricia (b.1924)   142
Belloc, Hilaire (1870–1953)   170
Berry, James (b.1924)   140
Betjeman, John (1906–84)   168
Binyon, Laurence (1869–1943)   103
Blunden, Edmund (1896–1974)   119
Bodecker, N. M. (b.1922)   123
Bridges, Robert (1844–1930)   122
Brock, Edwin (1927–97)   42
Brooke, Rupert (1887–1915)   144
Brown, George Mackay (b.1921)   79
Brownjohn, Alan (b. 1931)   40

Campbell, Roy (1902–57)   48
Causley, Charles (b.1917)   75
Chesterton, G. K. (1874–1936)   51
Clarke, Gillian (b.1937)   38
Coatsworth, Elizabeth (1893–1986)   121
Cope, Wendy (b.1945)   68
Cornford, Frances (1886–1960)   82
Crichton Smith, Iain (1925–98)   108
Cummings, E. E. (1894–1962)   114

Davies, W. H. (1871–1940)   34
Day Lewis, C. (1904–72)   90
De la Mare, Walter (1873–1956)   22
Doherty, Berlie (b.1943)   63
Douglas, Keith (1920–44)   150
Duffy, Carol Ann (b.1955)   175
Dunmore, Helen (b.1952)   156
Dunn, Douglas (b.1942)   97

Edwards, Richard (b.1949)   10
Eliot, T. S. (1888–1965)   128

Fanthorpe, U. A. (b.1929)   106
Farjeon, Eleanor (1881–1965)   56
Fatchen, Max (b.1920)   164
Fenton, James (b.1949)   159
Field, Rachel (1894–1942)   37
Flecker, James Elroy (1884–1915)   136
Frost, Robert (1874–1963)   132
Fuller, Roy (b.1912)   58

Gowar, Mick (b.1951)   165
Graves, Robert (1895–1985)   24
Gross, Philip (b.1952)   124
Gunn, Thom (b.1929)   35

Hamilton, Ian (b.1938)   144
Hardy, Thomas (1840–1928)   141
Harrison, Tony (b.1937)   85
Heaney, Seamus (b.1939)   84
Heath-Stubbs, John (b.1918)   30
Henri, Adrian (b.1932)   166
Hesketh, Phoebe (b.1909)   17
Hoban, Russell (b.1925)   15
Housman, A. E. (1859–1936)   72
Houston, Libby (b.1941)   113
Hughes, Langston (1902–67)   115
Hughes, Ted (1930–98)   45
Hulme, T. E. (1883–1917)   99

Jennings, Elizabeth (b.1926)   33
Jones, Brian (b.1938)   87
Joseph, Jenny (b.1932)   46

Kay, Jackie (b.1961)   66
Kipling, Rudyard (1865–1936)   145
Kirkup, James (b.1923)   153

Larkin, Philip (1922–85)   180
Lawrence, D. H. (1885–1930)   86
Lee, Brian (b.1935)   67
Lee, Laurie (1914–97)   116
Lindsay, Vachel (1879–1931)   53
Lochhead, Liz (b.1947)   80
Lowell, Robert (1917–77)   172
Lucie-Smith, Edward (b.1933)   83

MacBeth, George (b.1932)   126
MacCaig, Norman (1910–98)   52
McCord, David (1897–1997)   59
McGough, Roger (b.1937)   91
MacNeice, Louis (1907–63)   160
Masefield, John (1878–1967)   138
Mayer, Gerda (b.1927)   100
Mew, Charlotte (1870–1928)   161
Milne, A. A. (1882–1956)   120
Mitchell, Adrian (b.1932)   155
Mole, John (b.1941)   70
Morgan, Edwin (b.1920)   92
Morse, Brian (b.1948)   18
Muir, Edwin (1887–1959)   50
Muldoon, Paul (b.1951)   102

Nash, Ogden (1902–71) 60
Nicholls, Judith (b.1941) 28
Nichols, Grace (b.1950) 163
Nicholson, Norman (1914–87) 134
Noyes, Alfred (1880–1958) 176

Owen, Gareth (b.1936) 14
Owen, Wilfred (1893–1918) 147

Patten, Brian (b.1946) 164
Peake, Mervyn (1911–68) 109
Plath, Sylvia (1932–63) 26
Porter, Peter (b.1929) 151
Pound, Ezra (1885–1972) 162
Prelutsky, Jack (b.1940) 16
Pugh, Sheenagh (b.1950) 183

Raine, Craig (b.1944) 111
Raine, Kathleen (b.1908) 21
Reed, Henry (1914–86) 148
Reeves, James (1909–78) 139
Reid, Alastair (b.1926) 12
Rieu, E. V. (1887–1972) 44
Roethke, Theodore (1908–63) 36
Rosen, Michael (b.1946) 62
Ross, Alan (b.1922) 157

Sandburg, Carl (1878–1967) 120
Sassoon, Siegfried (1886–1967) 32
Scannell, Vernon (b.1922) 173
Serraillier, Ian (1912–94) 34
Silkin, Jon (1930–98) 54
Silverstein, Shel (b.1932) 11
Smith, Ken (b.1938) 130
Smith, Stevie (1902–71) 101
Spender, Stephen (b.1909) 78
Stallworthy, Jon (b.1935) 158
Stephens, James (1882–1950) 43
Summers, Hal (b.1911) 20
Sweeney, Matthew (b.1952) 94
Swenson, May (b.1919) 125

Tagore, Rabindranath (1861–1941) 77
Teasdale, Sara (1884–1933) 115
Thomas, Dylan (1914–53) 73
Thomas, Edward (1878–1917) 146
Thomas, R. S. (b.1913) 105

Wade, Barrie (b.1939) 65
Walcott, Derek (b.1930) 117
Walker, Ted (b.1934) 110
Weil, Zaro (b.?) 131
Williams, William Carlos (1883–1963) 47
Worth, Valerie (b.1935) 9
Wright, Judith (b.1915) 88
Wright, Kit (b.1944) 98

Yeats, W. B. (1865–1939) 182
Young, Andrew (1885–1971) 118

Index of Artists

Rebecca Gryspeerdt
pp17, 19, 36, 37, 61,
63, 64, 65, 68, 86, 107,
108, 114, 115, 120,
121, 126, 127, 157,
165, 167, 169

Hilary Paynter
pp21, 24, 25, 41, 43,
47, 52, 53, 59, 72, 75,
77, 82, 83, 95, 100,
101, 119, 132, 135,
145, 146, 181

Karen Perrins
pp2, 14, 15, 20, 22, 27,
28, 29, 30, 32, 39, 44,
45, 49, 51, 57, 73, 74,
78, 79, 82, 83, 85, 89,
92, 93, 98, 99, 102,
110, 117, 125, 131,
133, 138, 139, 151,
152, 154, 158, 159,
163, 164, 165, 172,
176, 177, 180, 182,
183, 188

Sarah Young
pp3, 9, 10, 13, 23, 33,
34, 35, 54, 55, 62, 63,
70, 71, 90, 91, 97, 112,
113, 123, 136, 137,
141, 143, 149, 161,
170, 171, 173, 174

Acknowledgements

Anna Adams: 'Unrecorded Speech' from *Bread and Roses* (Virago). Fleur Adcock: 'For a Five-year-old' from *Selected Poems* (OUP, 1983) by permission of Oxford University Press. John Agard: 'Don't Call Alligator Long-Mouth . . .' from *Say It Again, Granny* (Bodley Head) by permission of Random House UK Ltd. Allan Ahlberg: 'Where's Everybody?' from *Heard It in the Playground* (Viking, 1989), copyright © Allan Ahlberg 1989, by permission of Penguin Books Ltd. Maya Angelou: 'Televised' from *Collected Poems* (Virago), copyright © 1990 by Maya Angelou, by permission of Little Brown, London, and Random House, Inc. Simon Armitage: 'About His Person' from *Kid*, by permission of the publisher, Faber & Faber Ltd. W. H. Auden: 'O What is That Sound' from *The Collected Poems*, copyright © 1937 and renewed 1965 by W. H. Auden, by permission of the publishers, Faber & Faber Ltd and Random House, Inc. Michael Baldwin: 'Pitying Heaven' from *Hob and Other Poems* (Chatto). George Barker: 'They Call to One Another' from *To Aylsham Fair*, by permission of the publisher, Faber & Faber Ltd. Hilaire Belloc: 'Tarantella' from *Complete Verse* (Pimlico/Random), by permission of The Peters Fraser & Dunlop Group Limited on behalf of the Estate of Hilaire Belloc. Patricia Beer: 'Abbey Tomb' from *Collected Poems* (Carcanet, 1988), by permission of Carcanet Press Ltd. James Berry: 'Look, No Hands' from *Playing a Dazzler* (Hamish Hamilton, 1996), copyright © 1996 by James Berry, by permission of Penguin Books Ltd and Peters Fraser & Dunlop. John Betjeman: 'A Subaltern's Love-song' from *Collected Poems*, by permission of John Murray (Publishers) Ltd. Laurence Binyon: 'Hunger' from *Collected Poems* (Macmillan) by permission of The Society of Authors on behalf of the Laurence Binyon Estate. Edmund Blunden: 'The Midnight Skaters' from *Collected Poems* (Duckworth) by permission of The Peters Fraser & Dunlop Group Limited. N. M. Bodecker: 'When Skies are Low and Days are Dark' from *Snowman Sniffles*, copyright © 1983 by N. M. Bodecker, by permission of the publishers, Faber & Faber Ltd and Margaret K. McElderry Books, an imprint of Simon & Schuster Children's Publishing Division. Robert Bridges: 'London Snow' from *Poetical Works of Robert Bridges* (OUP, 1936) by permission of Oxford University Press. Edwin Brock: 'Song of the Battery Hen' from *Song of the Battery Hen* (Secker & Warburg) by permission of David Higham Associates. George Mackay Brown: 'A Child's Calendar' from *Selected Poems* by permission of John Murray (Publishers) Ltd. Alan Brownjohn: 'We are Going to See the Rabbit', copyright © Alan Brownjohn 1959, from *Collected Poems 1952–83* (Century Hutchinson) by permission of Rosica Colin Ltd. Roy Campbell: 'Horses on the Camargue' from *Adamastor* (Ad Donker), by permission of Jonathan Ball Publishers (Pty) Ltd. Charles Causley: 'By St Thomas Water' from *Union Street* (Macmillan) by permission of David Higham Associates. G. K. Chesterton: 'The Donkey' from *Collected Poems*, by permission of A. P. Watt Ltd on behalf of The Royal Literary Fund. Gillian Clarke: 'Trophy' from *PEN New Poetry II* (Quartet Books), copyright © English PEN, by permission of PEN. Elizabeth Coatsworth: 'On a Night of Snow' from *The Oxford Book of Children's Verse in America* (OUP). Wendy Cope: 'Tich Miller' from *Making Cocoa for Kingsley Amis*, by permission of the publisher, Faber & Faber Ltd. Frances Cornford: 'A Recollection' from *Collected Poems* (The Cresset Press), by permission of Random House UK Ltd. Iain Crichton Smith: 'Old Woman' from *Selected Poems* (Carcanet, 1985) by permission of Carcanet Press Ltd. E. E. Cummings: 'in Just-spring' from *Complete Poems 1904–1962* edited by George J. Firmage, copyright © 1991 by the Trustees for the E. E. Cummings Trust and George J. Firmage, by permission of the publishers, W. W. Norton & Company. W. H. Davies: 'The Example' from *Collected Poems* (Jonathan Cape), by permission of Random House UK Ltd. C. Day Lewis: 'Walking Away' from *The Complete Poems* (Sinclair-Stevenson, 1992), copyright © 1992 in this edition The Estate of C. Day Lewis, by permission of Random House UK Ltd. Walter de la Mare: 'The Listeners' from *Complete Poems* (UK, 1969/USA 1970), by permission of Literary Trustees of Walter de la Mare and The Society of Authors as their representative. Berlie Doherty: 'Playgrounds' from *Walking on Air* (Lion Publishing) by permission of David Higham Associates. Keith Douglas: 'Vergissmeinnicht' from *The Complete Poems* edited by Desmond Graham (3rd edition OUP, 1998) by permission of Oxford University Press. Carol Ann Duffy: 'Valentine' from *Meantime* (Anvil Press Poetry Ltd, 1993), by permission of the publisher. Helen Dunmore: 'In the Desert Knowing Nothing' from *Recovering a Body* (Bloodaxe Books, 1994) by permission of the publisher. Douglas Dunn: 'Men of Terry Street' from *Selected Poems*, by permission of the publisher, Faber & Faber Ltd. Richard Edwards: 'The Word Party' from *The Word Party* (Lutterworth Press/Puffin 1986/1987), by permission of the author. T. S. Eliot: 'Preludes' from *Collected Poems*, by permission of the publisher, Faber & Faber Ltd. **U. A. Fanthorpe**: 'Not My Best Side' from *Side Effects* (Peterloo, 1978), copyright © U. A. Fanthorpe 1978, by permission of the publisher. **Eleanor Farjeon**: 'It was Long Ago' from *Silver, Sand and Snow* (Michael Joseph) by permission of David Higham Associates. **Max Fatchen**: 'Lip Service' from *Wry Rhymes for Troublesome Times* (Kestrel Books, 1983), copyright © Max Fatchen 1983, by permission of John Johnson (Authors' Agent) Ltd. **James Fenton**: 'Tiananmen' [48 lines] from *Out of Danger* (Penguin) by permission of The Peters Fraser & Dunlop Group Limited. **Rachel Field**: 'Something Told the Wild Geese' from *Poems*, copyright holder not traced. **Robert Frost**: 'Mending Wall' from *The Poetry of Robert Frost* edited by Edward Connery Lathem (Jonathan Cape), copyright © 1969 by Henry Holt & Company, by permission of Random House UK Ltd on behalf of the Estate of Robert Frost. **Roy Fuller**: 'The Game of Life' from *Poor Roy* (Deutsch), by permission of John Fuller. **Mick Gowar**: 'Third Time Lucky' from *Third Time Lucky* (Viking), copyright © Mick Gowar, by permission of David Higham Associates. **Robert Graves**: 'Welsh Incident' from *Complete Poems, Volume 1* (Carcanet, 1995) by permission of Carcanet Press Ltd. **Philip Gross**: 'The Side Way Back' from *Scratch City*, by permission of the publisher, Faber & Faber Ltd **Thom Gunn**: 'Considering the Snail' from *My Sad Captains*, by permission of the publisher, Faber & Faber Ltd; also from *Collected Poems*, copyright © 1994 by Thom Gunn, by permission of Farrar Straus & Giroux, Inc. **Ian Hamilton**: 'Newscast' from *The Visit*, by permission of the publisher, Faber & Faber Ltd. **Tony Harrison**: 'The Icing Hand' from *The Gaze of the Gorgon* (Bloodaxe), by permission of Gordon Dickerson. **Seamus Heaney**: 'Follower' from *Death of a Naturalist*, by permission of the publisher, Faber & Faber Ltd; also from *Poems 1965–1975*, copyright © 1980 by Seamus Heaney, by permission of Farrar Straus & Giroux, Inc. **John Heath-Stubbs**: 'Great Black-Backed Gulls' from *Selected Poems* (Carcanet) by permission of David Higham Associates. **Adrian Henri**: 'Any prince to any princess' from *The Loveless Motel* (Jonathan Cape, 1979), copyright © 1979 Adrian Henri, by permission of the author c/o Rogers Coleridge & White Ltd, 20 Powis Mews, London W11 1JN. **Phoebe Hesketh**: 'The Frog Prince' from *Netting the Sun* (Enitharmon) by permission of the author. **Russell Hoban**: 'Not My Day' from *The Last of the Wallendas* (Heinemann) by permission of David Higham Associates. **A. E. Housman**: 'A Shropshire Lad, XL' ('Into my heart, an air . . .') from *Collected Poems* (Jonathan Cape) by permission of The Society of Authors as the Literary Representative of the Estate of A. E. Housman. **Libby Houston**: 'For the Record' from *All Change* (OUP) by permission of the author. **Langston Hughes**: 'April Rain Song' from *The Collected Poems of Langston Hughes* (Vintage US) by permission of David Higham Associates; also from *The Dream Keeper and Other Poems* (Knopf) copyright © 1994 by the Estate of Langston Hughes, by permission of Alfred A. Knopf, Inc. **Ted Hughes**: 'The Thought-Fox' from *Collected Poems* by permission of the publisher, Faber & Faber Ltd. **Elizabeth Jennings**: 'The Arrival of the Animals' from *Collected Poems* (Macmillan) by permission of David Higham Associates. **Brian Jones**: 'About Friends' from *Spitfire on the Northern Line* (Chatto & Windus), by permission of Random House UK Ltd. **Jenny Joseph**: 'Dog Body and Cat Mind' from *Selected Poems* (Bloodaxe, 1992), copyright © Jenny Joseph 1992, by permission of John Johnson (Authors' Agent) Ltd. **Jackie Kay**: 'Car Wash' from *Three Has Gone* (Blackie, 1994), copyright © Jackie Kay 1994, by permission of Penguin Books Ltd. **Rudyard Kipling**: 'My Boy Jack' from *Complete Poems* (Macmillan) by permission of A. P. Watt Ltd on behalf of The National Trust for Places of Historic Interest or Natural Beauty. **James Kirkup**: 'No More Hiroshimas' from *An Extended Breath: Collected Longer Poems and Sequences* (University of Salzburg Press, 1996), by permission of the author. **Philip Larkin**: 'An Arundel Tomb' from *Collected Poems*, copyright © 1988, 1989 by the Estate of Philip Larkin, by permission of the publishers, Faber & Faber Ltd and Farrar Straus & Giroux, Inc. **D. H. Lawrence**: 'Piano' from *The Complete Poems of D. H. Lawrence* edited by V. de Sola Pinto & F. W. Roberts, copyright © 1964, 1971 by Angelo Ravagli and C. M. Weekley, Executors of the Estate of Frieda Lawrence Ravagli, by permission of Laurence Pollinger Limited, the Estate of Frieda Lawrence Ravagli, and Viking Penguin, a division of Penguin Putnam Inc. **Brian Lee**: 'The Tunnel' from *Late Home* (Kestrel Books, 1976), copyright © 1976 by Brian Lee, by permission of Penguin Books Ltd. **Laurie Lee**: 'Day of These Days' from *Selected Poems* (Penguin) by permission of The Peters Fraser & Dunlop Group Limited. **Vachel Lindsay**: 'The Flower-Fed Buffaloes' from *Going to the Stars* (A Hawthorn Book), copyright 1926 by D. Appleton & Co., renewed © 1954 by Elizabeth C. Lindsay, by permission of Dutton Children's Books, a division of Penguin Putnam Inc. **Liz Lochhead**: 'Revelation' from *Dreaming Frankenstein and Collected Poems* (Polygon), by permission of the publisher. **Robert Lowell**: 'Water' from *Selected Poems*, by permission of the publisher, Faber & Faber Ltd; also from *For the Union Dead*, copyright © 1959 by Robert Lowell, copyright © renewed 1987 by Harriet Lowell, Caroline Lowell, and Sheridan Lowell, by permission of Farrar, Straus & Giroux, Inc. **Edward Lucie-Smith**: 'The Lesson' from *A Tropical Childhood and Other Poems* (OUP, 1961),

'Father Says' from *Mind Your Own Business* (1974), by permission of Andre Deutsch Children's Books, an imprint of Scholastic Ltd. **Alan Ross**: 'Carriers in the Gulf' from *After Pusan* (Harvill Press, 1996), by permission of the author. **Carl Sandburg**: 'Fog' from *Chicago Poems*, copyright 1916 by Holt, Rinehart & Winston and renewed © 1944 by Carl Sandburg, by permission of Harcourt Brace & Company. **Siegfried Sassoon**: 'Everyone Sang' from *Collected Poems of Siegfried Sassoon* (Robson Books/Dutton), copyright 1920 by E. P. Dutton, copyright © renewed 1948 by Siegfried Sassoon, by permission of George Sassoon and Viking Penguin, a division of Penguin Putnam Inc. **Vernon Scannell**: 'No Sense of Direction' from *Collected Poems*, by permission of the author. **Ian Serraillier**: 'The Tickle Rhyme' from *The Monster Horse* (OUP, 1950), by permission of Mrs Anne Serraillier. **Jon Silkin**: 'Caring for Animals' from *Selected Poems* (Routledge). **Shel Silverstein**: 'Whatif' from *A Light in the Attic* (Cape), copyright © 1981 by Evil Eye Music, Inc., by permission of the Edite Kroll Literary Agency and HarperCollins Publishers, Inc. **Ken Smith**: 'Encounter at St Martin's' from *Terra* (Bloodaxe, 1986) by permission of the publisher. **Stevie Smith**: 'Not Waving but Drowning' from *The Collected Poems of Stevie Smith* (Penguin 20th Century Classics), copyright © 1972 by Stevie Smith, by permission of New Directions Publishing Corp and James MacGibbon. **Stephen Spender**: 'Lost Days' from *The Generous Days*, copyright © 1971 by Stephen Spender, by permission of the publishers, Faber & Faber Ltd and Random House, Inc. **Jon Stallworthy**: 'A Poem about Poems about Vietnam' from *Root and Branch* (Chatto & Windus), by permission of Random House UK Ltd. **James Stephens**: 'The Snare', by permission of The Society of Authors as the Literary Representative of the Estate of James Stephens. **Hal Summers**: 'A Spell for Midnight' from *Selected Poems* (OUP), by permission of the author. **Matthew Sweeney**: 'Resurrected' from *Fatso in the Red Suit*, by permission of the publisher, Faber & Faber Ltd. **May Swenson**: 'Southbound on the Freeway' from *The Complete Poems to Solve*, copyright © 1993 The Literary Estate of May Swenson (originally published in *The New Yorker*, 1963), by permission of Simon & Schuster Books for Young Readers, an imprint of Simon & Schuster Children's Publishing Division. **Rabindranath Tagore**: 'I Wish I Were . . .' from *Collected Poems* (Nelson), copyright © Visva-Bharati, by permission of Visva-Bharati University, Calcutta. **Sara Teasdale**: 'There Will Come Soft Rains' from *Collected Poems* by permission of Wellesley College Library, Special Collections. **Dylan Thomas**: 'Fern Hill' from *Collected Poems* (Dent) by permission of David Higham Associates. **R. S. Thomas**: 'Evans' from *Selected Poems* (Granada Publishing) by permission of the author. **Barrie Wade**: 'Truth' from *Conkers* (OUP) by permission of the author. **Derek Walcott**: 'Midsummer, Tobago' from *Sea Grapes* (Jonathan Cape), by permission of Random House UK Ltd and from *Collected Poems 1948–1984* copyright © 1986 by Derek Walcott, by permission of the publishers, Farrar Straus & Giroux, Inc. **Ted Walker**: 'The Doomed Spaceman' from *Grandad's Seagulls* (Blackie), copyright © Ted Walker 1965, by permission of Sheil Land Associates. **Zaro Weil**: 'Shadows' from *Mud, Moon and Me* (first published in the UK in 1989 by Orchard Books, a division of the Watts Publishing Group, 96 Leonard Street, London EC2A 4RH), by permission of the publisher. **William Carlos Williams**: 'Poem' from *Collected Poems: 1909–1939*, Volume 1, copyright © 1938 by New Directions Publishing Corp., by permission of the publishers; also from *Collected Poems: Volume 1* (Carcanet, 1987) by permission of Carcanet Press Ltd. **Valerie Worth**: 'library' from *Small Poems Again*, copyright © 1986 by Valerie Worth, by permission of Farrar Straus & Giroux, Inc **Judith Wright**: 'Legend' from *A Human Pattern: Selected Poems* (ETT Imprint, 1996) by permission of the publisher. **Kit Wright**: 'Every Day in Every Way' from *Poems 1974–83* (Hutchinson) by permission of the author. **W. B. Yeats**: 'He Wishes for the Cloths of Heaven' from *The Collected Works of W. B. Yeats Vol. 1: The Poems*, revised and edited by Richard J. Finneran, copyright © 1983, 1989 by Anne Yeats, by permission of Scribner, a Division of Simon & Schuster and A. P. Watt Ltd on behalf of Michael B. Yeats. **Andrew Young**: 'Hard Frost' from *Selected Poems* (Carcanet, 1998) by permission of Carcanet Press Ltd.

Although every effort has been made to trace and contact copyright holders before publication, this has not been possible in every case. If notified, the publisher will be pleased to rectify any errors or omissions at the earliest opportunity.